CONTENTS

Preface	v
Introduction	1
Introduction to an International Company	3
You and Fun & Games International	5
Pre-Activity Application for the Job	6
Enrichment A: Application Process	7
Enrichment B: Preparation for an Interview	8
Enrichment C: Interview Preparation	9
You Got the Job!	11

JOB 1 — ONE-PAGE MEMO: ORGANIZATION OF INTERNATIONAL MARKETS — 13

Enrichment Activity: FGI Organizational Chart — 14

JOB 2 — TABLE: EXPORT TERMS — 15

Enrichment Activity: Review of Export Terms — 17

JOB 3 — ONE-PAGE REPORT: INTERNATIONAL TELEPHONE CALLS — 19

Enrichment Activity: Time Zones — 21

JOB 4 — BLOCK LETTER: SERVICE CENTER PURPOSE AND PROCEDURES — 23

Enrichment Activity: Review of Service Center Procedures — 25

JOB 5 — TWO-PAGE REPORT: LATIN AMERICAN CULTURE — 27

Enrichment Activity: Cultural Diversity — 31

JOB 6 — TABLE: ORDER/SHIPPING PROCESS FOR MEXICO — 33

Enrichment Activity: A Matter of Ethics — 34

Contents iii

JOB 7	**MEMO WITH REFERENCE SHEET: EXPORT EFFORTS AND MISTAKES**	**37**
	Enrichment Activity: Language and Proofreading Skills (Swahili—A Trade Language)	39
	Performance Review	**41**
	Production Problem Rating Guide	**42**
JOB 8	**TWO-PAGE REPORT: AFRICAN CULTURE**	**43**
	Enrichment Activity: Currency Exchange Rates	45
JOB 9	**LETTER WITH TABLE: ORDER CONFIRMATION**	**47**
	Enrichment Activity: Ethnic Foods in the United States	48
JOB 10	**TABLE AND ONE-PAGE REPORT: TRAVEL ASSISTANCE**	**50**
	Enrichment Activity: Geography Review	52
JOB 11	**FORM LETTERS: SERVICE CENTERS AND ACCOUNTS PAYABLE**	**54**
	Enrichment Activity: Slang Expressions	57
JOB 12	**THREE-PAGE REPORT: JAPANESE CULTURE**	**59**
	Enrichment Activity: Cultural Review	63
JOB 13	**TWO TABLES: JAPANESE HOLIDAYS AND TOURIST ATTRACTIONS**	**65**
	Enrichment Activity: Ethnic Holidays and Celebrations in the United States	67
JOB 14	**TWO-PAGE MEMO: GREETINGS AND BUSINESS CARDS**	**69**
	Enrichment Activity: Foreign Language Vocabulary	71

Performance Review — **73**
Production Problem Rating Guide — **74**
Reference Manual — 75

FUN & GAMES

INTERNATIONAL

A KEYBOARDING SIMULATION

C.B. STIEGLER, Ed.D.
Northern Kentucky University

South-Western Publishing Co.

Copyright © 1995
by SOUTH-WESTERN PUBLISHING CO.
Cincinnati, Ohio

ALL RIGHTS RESERVED

The text of this publication, or any part thereof, may not be reproduced or transmitted in any form or by any means, electronic or mechanical, including photocopying, recording, storage in an information retrieval system, or otherwise, without the prior written permission of the publisher.

Library of Congress Cataloging-in-Publication Data

Stiegler, C. B.
    Fun & games international : a keyboarding simulation / C.B. Stiegler.
       p. cm.
   ISBN 0–538–62345–4
   1. Business--Data processing—Problems, exercises, etc.
2. International business enterprises—Data processing—Problems, exercises, etc. 3. Electronic data processing—Keyboarding--Problems, exercises, etc. 4. Business communication--Simulation methods. I. Title. II. Title: Fun and games international.
HF5548.2.S793 1995
651.8--dc20   93-40862
                                                                                                         CIP

ISBN: 0-538-62345-4

6 7 8 BAW 00 99 98

Printed in the United States of America

I(T)P
International Thomson Publishing

South-Western Publishing Co. is an ITP Company. The ITP trademark is used under license

Executive Editor: Karen Schmohe
Developmental Editor: Richard E. Adams
Coordinating Editor: Susan Richardson
Production Manager: Deborah M. Luebbe
Senior Production Editor: Jane Congdon
Marketing Manager: Al S. Roane
Design: South-Western Publishing Co.

PREFACE

INTRODUCTION

Because most businesses and consumers in the United States are involved in or affected by a global economy, this simulation will help prepare you to be a more knowledgeable citizen and a more effective employee. In addition to studying facets of international business while using your keyboarding skills, you will also be able to reinforce your basic abilities in reading, writing, math, and problem solving.

ACKNOWLEDGMENTS

Even though Fun & Games International is not a real company, the Jobs provide good examples of the information processing that might exist in an actual company. The author of this simulation is grateful to two executives from Kenner Toys for their help in this project: Mr. Corky Steiner, vice president, Latin American Division, and Mr. Terry Bernard, director of Creative Services.

Special appreciation goes to Mr. James Kent Stiegler, General Services Officer, U.S. Department of State—Chad, Africa, and Bern, Switzerland—and to Mrs. Karen Brown Stiegler, freelance journalist, for their assistance with cultural information. Acknowledgment and appreciation also go to Mrs. Marilyn Sarch for her editorial suggestions.

FEATURES

The simulation is organized so that you can do the Jobs at your own pace, with an overall time frame for the beginning and completion of the simulation established by your teacher. You will assume a part-time position and do the work that would be expected of a person employed by a company. You are also expected to use good work habits and to show others that you want to learn, that you respect them, and that you take pride in what you do.

For each job, you are given needed supplies, Reference Manual sources, and specific instructions for completion of your work. Each job can be completed on a typewriter or on information processing equipment with word processing software. The Reference Manual at the end of the simulation provides guidelines for formats.

After each Job, you are given an Enrichment Activity. These activities will help you learn more about—or reinforce information about—international business and communication. They are also designed to help you refine your research, math, and problem-solving skills.

With many Jobs, you are given additional information about international business and communication. These information bits are titled FYI (For Your Information). The FYIs are provided for the purposes of individual reading and/or group discussion. Share them with your friends and family.

INSTRUCTIONS

1. Begin by reading these sections:

    Introduction

    Introduction to an International Company

    You and Fun & Games International

2. Read and complete Pre-Activity Application for the Job—be sure to follow the instructions and to study the application letter example.

3. Give your completed letter and its addressed envelope to your teacher.

4. Complete three Enrichment Activities:

    Enrichment Activity A: Application Process

    Enrichment Activity B: Preparation for an Interview

    Enrichment Activity C: Interview Preparation

5. For each of the remaining 14 Jobs and Enrichment Activities, follow the instructions given in YOU GOT THE JOB.

INTRODUCTION

A Global Economy

The global marketplace is here! People in the United States buy Japanese cars and electronics, Italian shoes, Philippine underwear, Hong Kong watches, and Taiwan clothing. Such goods and services made in another country but sold in the United States are known as **imports**.

Goods and services made in the United States but sold to other countries are **exports**. Businesses in the United States export a wide variety of products—food, beverages, high-tech goods, and cars are examples.

United States businesses not only transport goods and services to other countries, they also set up businesses and offices in other countries. For example, McDonald's restaurants are in Moscow, Beijing, Budapest, Frankfurt, and Glasgow. Another example is Reebok International Ltd.; it set up its first specialty store in Moscow in 1993 and agreed to outfit the Russian Olympic athletes from 20 sports federations in Reebok footwear and clothing through the 1996 Summer Olympic Games in Atlanta, GA.

In addition to transporting goods and services to the United States, businesses from other countries also set up offices and industries in the United States. For example, Japanese automobile manufacturers have established auto assembly plants in several states:

Manufacturer	State
Honda	East Liberty, OH
	Marysville, OH
Mazda (with Ford)	Flat Rock, MI
Mitsubishi (with Chrysler)	Normal, IL
Nissan	Smyrna, TN
Subaru-Isuzu	Lafayette, IN
Toyota	Georgetown, KY
Toyota (with General Motors)	Fremont, CA

Such a global marketplace is possible, in large part, because of advancements in technology (computers, telephones, fax machines) and transportation (planes, trains, ships). Technology and transportation make it easier to manufacture products, create services, and buy and sell both. They also make it easier for countries to talk with one another and to make agreements to support or restrict trade within their boundaries. For example, the United States is part of the North American Free Trade Agreement, whereby Canada, Mexico and the United States agree to eliminate barriers to trade in goods and services and to ease restrictions on cross-border investments.

Introduction 1

Paris is part of the global marketplace.

Not only are people doing business in a global economic setting, but they are also living and working with people who have different cultural backgrounds. For example, in the United States there are many company employees from Europe, Africa, Mexico, Asia, and the Middle East who are American citizens. This mixture of people from various cultures is known as **cultural diversity**.

Not only are you part of a global economy as a consumer but you are also part of a global social environment. You go to school, socialize, and work with people who have different cultural heritages. Your career will probably include positions with companies that conduct business internationally, employ a culturally diverse work force, and provide products and services to culturally diverse consumers.

With a global marketplace and a culturally diverse work force, everyone needs to understand and appreciate cultural differences. We also need to be able to communicate respectfully and effectively. Businesses today value workers who can work with people who have varied cultural backgrounds; they value workers who can provide quality service to customers who have varied cultural backgrounds.

Because you are part of a global economy and social environment, this simulation will give you information about various cultures and a better understanding of information processing activities in a business setting.

Specifically, in this simulation, you will:

1. Apply keyboarding and word processing skills.
2. Integrate and apply basic skills in math, reading, and writing.
3. Learn the vocabulary used in international business.
4. Develop an awareness of other cultures and languages.
5. Apply decision-making and communication skills for trade documentation.
6. Refine employability skills.
7. Have a better understanding of international travel.
8. Understand and appreciate cultural diversity.

INTRODUCTION TO AN INTERNATIONAL COMPANY

Fun & Games

In 1950, Mark Webster and Barbara Wehir created the board game Wizard Math. They played it with friends, gave it as presents, donated it to groups for door prizes, and eventually had customers calling to buy the game. That one product was the beginning of Fun & Games.

A successful board game was the beginning of FGI.
Photo Credit: H. Armstrong Roberts

Cultural Expansion

From 1950 to 1970, Fun & Games developed other games, puzzles, and toys and sold all of its products in the United States. In the 70's, Fun & Games found it hard to increase its sales in the United States because there was so much competition and only so many consumers.

With transportation and communication around the world becoming easier and less expensive, the company decided to expand outside the United States to sell its products. By studying the life-styles of people in other cultures, it identified appropriate games, toys, and puzzles. The company translated the names, instructions and content of the selected products into the language of each targeted country.

Fun & Games recognized the importance of getting to know a country and its people in order to sell its products and services. It knew that what sold well in the United

States might not do as well elsewhere unless changes were made to account for different cultural factors and needs.

With its move to market products outside the United States, Fun & Games became a **multinational company** (a company that does business not only in the United States but also in other countries). In recognition of its step into a global economy, Fun & Games formally changed its name to Fun & Games International (FGI).

Culturally Diverse Work Force

Over the years, FGI's business has grown steadily. When FGI moved into the global marketplace, its management made a commitment to achieve three goals:

1. Recruit and employ people with varied cultural backgrounds.
2. Train its people to be sensitive to cultural differences.
3. Acquaint its workers with the vocabulary and procedures used in international business.

FGI is proud that its work force today is culturally diverse. People have been hired because of their cultural knowledge, job-related skills, and ability to be team players for FGI. The company supports its employees by offering training programs and reading materials to help them appreciate and acquire the skills necessary to be successful in a global market.

FGI managers in international offices and plants must come from—or know—particular cultures to effectively supervise employees and to serve local customers. The company recognizes that an understanding of other cultures and their languages helps in the development and selling of products and services.

YOU AND FUN & GAMES INTERNATIONAL

YOUR SKILLS

Since you know the keyboard and can now format (correctly set up and key) letters, memos, tables, and reports, you have a skill that you can use to earn money in business. Keyboarding skills are used to process information in business (letters and reports, for example) and in our personal lives (letters, resumes, school reports, and notes, for example).

JOB POSTING

Fun & Games International has hired co-op students from your school. So when they need part-time workers, they give a job ad to your school's co-op supervisor so it can be posted on the bulletin board. You see the following job description on the board:

```
                PART-TIME TYPING/WORD PROCESSING

Multinational company seeks person with keyboarding
and formatting skills for part-time position.  Must
be detail-oriented, a self-starter, and able to work
with information and people from a variety of
cultures.  On-the-job training in international
business skills is available.  Flexible hours
available.
                        Equal Opportunity Employer
        See School Co-op Coordinator for Employer Contact
```

PRE-ACTIVITY

APPLICATION FOR THE JOB

INSTRUCTIONS

Use the example application letter as a guide to write a letter to FGI to apply for the position.

Key the letter using plain paper.

Include your return address.

Use today's date.

Address the letter to:
Ms. Paula Hougen
Vice President of Personnel
Fun & Games International
425 Fourth Street
P.O. Box 2000
Cincinnati, OH 45202-2000

You decide to apply for the part-time typing/word processing position at Fun & Games International. You talk with the co-op teacher, who gives you an example of an application letter and the instructions at the left.

```
Street Address
City, State ZIP
Current Date   line 16
```

Inside Address   line 20

Dear   line 26 (or DS below inside address—depends on length of address)

After seeing your ad for a person to do part-time typing and word processing, I talked with the co-op teacher here at (give the name of your school). I believe I have the skills you need in this position, and I would appreciate your consideration of me for this job.

During this year, I have taken (give the name of your typing, keyboarding or word processing course) at (give the name of your high school). I can type (give the number of words) words per minute, and I know how to format letters, memos, tables and reports. You can depend on me to follow instructions and to check my work carefully.

In my business classes, I have also studied about our global economy. I do know the importance of showing respect for people from other cultures, and I have become aware of culture differences. Even though I do not have a lot of experience in working with people from a lot of different cultures, I do learn quickly and am really interested in working with people and products in international business.

At your convenience, I would like to talk with you about the skills that I could bring to this job. Could I please have an interview? I can be reached at (give your telephone number including your area code).

Sincerely yours

Strike return key four times

(key your name)

ENRICHMENT ACTIVITY A

APPLICATION PROCESS

INSTRUCTIONS

Your co-op teacher gives you an application from Fun & Games International. Complete the application form—properly align and key the information requested.

Enrichment Activity A

ENRICHMENT ACTIVITY B — PREPARATION FOR AN INTERVIEW

INSTRUCTIONS

Important words from Fun & Games International's job ad are listed here. Using your school courses and activities, work experiences, volunteer and/or organizational activities, list examples that you could mention to show you have the characteristics they desire in the person they hire.

Characteristic	Personal Example
Keyboarding Skill	_____
Formatting Skill	_____
Detail-Oriented	_____
Self-Starter	_____
Able to Work with Culturally Diverse People	_____
Able to Work with Culturally Diverse Information	_____

What could you do if you do not have anything to list for one of the characteristics?

_____

Enrichment Activity B

ENRICHMENT ACTIVITY C

INTERVIEW PREPARATION

INSTRUCTIONS

1. Read the three classified advertisements for positions with international companies.
2. Using the space provided, answer the questions following the advertisements.

Secretary—Part-Time Position
International company seeks bilingual person (English & Spanish) for telephone screening, word processing, and filing. Must have good verbal and organizational skills and be self-motivated. 15–20 hours per week. EEOC. 282-4523
Ad #1

Wanted—Word Processor
Skilled word processors & typists needed for multinational firm. Must be able to produce documents from rough draft copy, answer multi-line phones, and do filing. Good grammar a must! Free training on variety of software products. Call 721-8365.
Ad #2

Word Processor—Part-Time Hours!
Non-smoking office seeks Word Processor. DOS/WINDOWS ENVIRONMENT. Experience in word processing. Minimum 60 wpm. Needs to be organized, flexible, dependable. Must be a team player. Send resume to PM Company, Dept. HR221 24 Triangle Park Drive, Tampa, FL 33619.
Ad #3

What are the desirable traits mentioned in each advertisement?

Ad #1: _____
_____
_____

Ad #2: _____
_____
_____

Ad #3: _____
_____
_____

What skill is mentioned in all the advertisements? _____

Enrichment Activity C

Write your explanation of the following phrases/words:

Telephone Screening _____

_____

Self-Motivated _____

_____

Rough Draft _____

Multi-Line Phones _____

_____

Team Player _____

_____

YOU GOT THE JOB!

Congratulations! You got the job and are ready to work. Begin by reading the instructions below:

INSTRUCTIONS

1. You are working for James Story, Director of International Sales, doing typing/word processing jobs. See the Organizational Chart on page 76.

2. As you prepare to do each Job, read the instructions carefully. Begin with Job 1 (unless your instructor gives you other directions).

3. Use FGI's Reference Manual on pages 75–88 for instructions on formats and procedures.

4. At the end of each Job you will find an Enrichment Activity which will help you build your insights and skills for working in multi-national companies and living in a global social environment. Unless your instructor gives you other directions, carefully read each activity. As you follow instructions, be sure to write legibly, neatly, and correctly. Such habits will make it easier for people who have English as a second language to read the content.

5. Carefully proofread each completed Job and correct all errors. Be sure it is neat and accurate. The documents you produce are part of the professional image of FGI!

6. Be sure to key your name, the Job number, the date, and any other information your instructor directs at the top of each paper you prepare.

7. Submit completed Jobs according to your instructor's directions. You may be asked to submit each Job as you complete it or to submit at the end of the period all Jobs completed during that class period.

JOB 1
ONE-PAGE MEMO: ORGANIZATION OF INTERNATIONAL MARKETS

SUPPLIES

Plain Paper or Memo Form

REFERENCE MANUAL

Organizational Chart
Proofreader's Marks
Formal Memo Format

INSTRUCTIONS

Key memo shown here on plain paper.

Use a 1" or default margin.

Put your initials (lower-case) a double space below the body of the memo.

TO: Antonio Villas, Director, Sales Administration
FROM: James Story, Director, International Sales
DATE: *use current date*
SUBJECT: Organization of International Markets

To make it easier for *your* people to quickly identify our sales managers and their territories, I suggest we give them the following clarification of our organizational chart. *respective* / *tr*

Sales Manager	Territory
Rigalli	
Pellegrini	European community — France, Belgium, Italy, Greece, Germany, Denmark, Spain, United Kingdom, Netherlands, Ireland, Portugal, Luxembourg
Dean	
Chan	Asia — Singapore, South Korea, Taiwan, Hong Kong, Japan

This clarifies the countries that are included in the european community and in the pacific rim. Using a table format such as this will make it easier for your customer service staff to quickly answer any questions about who is responsible for particular countries. If I can help you with anything else, just let me know.

xxx

Get complete names and territories from original chart — double space between listings

Put countries in European Community and in Asia in alphabetical order

JOB 1

SUPPLIES
This Page

♦

INSTRUCTIONS
Refer to the Organizational Chart in your FGI Reference Manual to answer the following questions in the spaces provided below.

ENRICHMENT ACTIVITY

FGI ORGANIZATIONAL CHART

1. The three directors who report to Mr. Kupper are:

   _____

   _____

   _____

2. Who is the person responsible for East Coast Sales?

   _____

3. To whom does the above person report?

   _____

4. To whom does Betty Locklear report?

   _____

5. The two people who report to Antonio Villas are:

   _____

   _____

6. The persons on the same organizational level as Mr. Kupper are:

   _____

   _____

7. List the people on the same organizational level as Ms. Locklear.

   _____

   _____

8. The Manager of Computer Operations is _____.

9. Identify the two directors who report to Neal Bulla.

   _____

   _____

14 …………………………………………………………………………… JOB 1 • Enrichment Activity

JOB 2
TABLE: EXPORT TERMS

SUPPLIES
Plain Paper

REFERENCE MANUAL
Table Format
Proofreader's Marks

INSTRUCTIONS
Key these terms/definitions in a two-column table, using 1" top and side or default margins.

Title the table: FREQUENTLY USED EXPORTING TERMS.

Arrange the terms in alphabetical order.

Leave 4 spaces between columns.

Export Term	Definition
Quotation	An offer to sell goods at a stated price and under specific conditions.
Correspondent bank	A bank that in its own country handles the business of a foreign bank.
Devaluation	The official lowering of the value of one country's currency in terms of one or more foreign currencies.
Tare weight	Weight of a container and packing materials without the weight of the goods it contains.
Eximbank	The Export-Import Bank of the U.S.
Exchange rate	Price of one currency in terms of another.
Distributor	Foreign agent who sells directly for a supplier and keeps an inventory of the supplier's products.
Political risk	Risk of loss due to possible government action preventing entry of goods, government takeover of property/goods, or restrictions on money exchange.
Free trade zone	Port approved by the government of a country for duty-free entry of nonprohibited goods. Goods can be stored, displayed, or used for manufacturing within zone.
Ship's manifest	List of ship's cargo; list is signed by captain of the ship.
Bill of lading	Document showing terms of contract between a shipper and a transportation company. It is prepared by the carrier.
Asian dollars	U.S. dollars deposited in Asian banks.

(Continued on next page)

FYI

HONG KONG

In 1841, Hong Kong was created as a tiny British colony. In 1984, Britain and China signed a joint declaration that would end Hong Kong's ties with Britain. At midnight, June 30, 1997, Hong Kong will become a Special Administrative Region of the People's Republic of China.
Hong Kong has a large harbor and is a focal point in shipping goods to the world's marketplaces.

Eurodollars	U.S. dollars on deposit in European banks.
Customs	Authorities that collect duties (fees) on imports and exports.
Duty	A tax imposed on imports by the customs authority of a country.

16 .... JOB 2 • Table: Export Terms

JOB 2

ENRICHMENT ACTIVITY

REVIEW OF EXPORT TERMS

SUPPLIES
This Page

INSTRUCTIONS
Without looking at the table you keyed, see how many terms you can recall by writing them in the appropriate blanks.

1. A bank in the United States which handles the business of a bank in Germany is known as a _____ bank.

2. The captain of a ship signs a document which lists the cargo of the ship. That listing is the ship's _____ .

3. United States dollars deposited in a bank in Frankfort, Germany, are _____ dollars.

4. If the value of the dollar goes down in comparison to Germany's currency (deutsche mark), the term used to explain this process is _____ .

5. Goods coming into the United States may be taxed by the customs authority; this is called a _____ .

6. If a company thinks that the government of a foreign country may take over its plants in that foreign country, it is a _____ risk for that company.

7. The contract between a shipper and a transportation company is a _____ .

8. The full weight of a container, including packing, without the weight of the goods is known as _____ weight.

9. A port where goods can be stored or displayed duty free is a _____ zone.

10. Dollars in a Japanese bank are known as _____ dollars.

JOB 2 • Enrichment Activity 17

11. The authorities who collect duties on imports and/or exports are known as _____ authorities.

12. If a U. S. company hires a German businessperson to sell directly for it and to keep an inventory in Germany, this person is known as a _____.

13. A _____ is an offer to sell goods at a stated price and under specific conditions.

14. If someone asked you the price of the dollar in terms of the New peso (Mexican dollar), that person would be asking you for the _____ of the dollar.

15. The Export-Import Bank of the United States is known as _____.

JOB 3

ONE-PAGE REPORT: INTERNATIONAL TELEPHONE CALLS

SUPPLIES

One Plain Sheet of Paper

REFERENCE MANUAL

Report Format

INSTRUCTIONS

Key the information here as a one-page report.

Use 1" or default margins.

Title it: **TELEPHONE COMMUNICATION IN INTERNATIONAL TIME ZONES.**

Use side headings.

A knowledge of time zones and techniques for direct dialing will help you to be cost effective in placing international telephone calls.

Time Zone Considerations

Each employee must be aware of domestic and international time zones before placing a call. Making calls during regular business hours in particular countries will help eliminate "telephone tag"—making several calls to try to talk to someone.

There are 24 time zones around the world. The time zones for the United States—Eastern, Central, Mountain, Pacific—are shown in telephone books. A chart of international time zones is provided in FGI's reference manual. As you look at the time zone chart, notice that from the Eastern time zone in the U.S. you would add 6 hours for a call to Germany, 7 hours for a call to South Africa, and 13 hours for a call to Hong Kong.

(Continued on next page)

FYI

24-HOUR TIME

24-hour time is widely used in scientific work throughout the world. In the U.S., it is used also by the Armed Forces. In Europe, it is used frequently by the transportation networks.

Midnight	0000 Hours
1 a.m.	0100
2 a.m.	0200
3 a.m.	0300
7 a.m.	0700
Noon	1200
1 p.m.	1300
3 p.m.	1500
8 p.m.	2000
10 p.m.	2200
11 p.m.	2300

Direct Dialing

International calling directions are given in your local telephone book. Use four steps to direct-dial an international call — dial the International Access Code (11), the Country Code, the City Code, and then the local telephone number. For example, for a call to Frankfurt, Germany, you would dial 11 (International Access Code), 49 (Country Code), 69 (Frankfurt City Code), and the local number there.

JOB 3

ENRICHMENT ACTIVITY — TIME ZONES

SUPPLIES
This Page

REFERENCE MANUAL
International Time Zone Chart

Domestic Time Zone Map

3–1 INSTRUCTIONS
See how much you can recall about time zones from the one-page report you just keyed by answering the review questions.

3–2 INSTRUCTIONS
Identify the country location for each of the cities listed on page 22.

Using the International Time Zones Chart in the Reference Manual, figure what time it is in the listed cities when it is 9 a.m. in Cincinnati, OH; 2 p.m. in Wichita, KS; and 4:30 p.m. in Fresno, CA.

Using the Domestic Time Zones Map, calculate what time it is in the listed cities in the United States when it is 9 a.m. in Cincinnati, OH; 2 p.m. in Wichita, KS; and 4:30 p.m. in Fresno, CA.

Review

1. How many times zones are there in the United States?

   _____

2. How many time zones are there around the world?

   _____

3. Where can you find a map of the international time zones in the United States?

   _____

4. If you are going to direct-dial an international number, how many steps are there?

   _____

5. What are the steps for direct dialing an international number?

   _____

   _____

   _____

JOB 3 • Enrichment Activity   21

CALCULATIONS FOR INTERNATIONAL TIME ZONES

City	Country	9 a.m. Cincinnati	2 p.m. Wichita	4:30 p.m. Fresno
Rio de Janeiro	Brazil	11 a.m.	5 p.m.	9:30 p.m.
Buenos Aires				
Beijing				
San Jose				
New Delhi				
Dublin				
Mexico City				
Lima				
Moscow				
Cape Town				
Bangkok				

CALCULATIONS FOR DOMESTIC TIME ZONES

City	State	9 a.m. Cincinnati	2 p.m. Wichita	4:30 p.m. Fresno
Flagstaff				
Atlanta				
Juneau				
Sioux City				
Lubbock				

JOB 4
BLOCK LETTER: SERVICE CENTER PURPOSE AND PROCEDURES

SUPPLIES
Plain Paper or Letterhead

REFERENCE MANUAL
Letter Format
Proofreader's Marks

INSTRUCTIONS
Key letter in block format.

Begin with current date on plain paper or letterhead.

Put date on line 13 since this is a long letter.

Supply the proper salutation.

Key James Story, Director, International Sales as the sender.

Use your initials to show who keyed the document.

Señor
Mr. Granjas Estrella
G. E. Electronics
Tapachula 96
Tijuana, B. C. Mexico

Dear Mr. Estrella — Congratulations, Señor Estrella.
Señor

G.E. Electronics is designated as the Service Center for the repair of FGI electronic toys and games. Having such a service center will help FGI keep customers satisfied through quick quick service. And, since the center is local, it will be less expensive for FGI to maintain quality products in Mexico.

The Service Center is expected to provide these services:

1. Verify warranty coverage before service is rendered.
2. Provide service in a prompt, efficient and workmanlike manner.
3. Use genuine FGI parts to service electronic games and toys.
4. Under no circumstances will it alter, modify, or delete original circuitry of any product (except as directed by FGI).
5. Notify FGI immediately, in writing, if any FGI product does not meet consumer product safety requirements.
6. Submit full and complete in-warranty reports to FGI.
7. Keep up to date on FGI developments and service techniques.
8. Appove periodic visits by FGI to discuss level of support.

FGI will provide the service center with manuals and parts for service. If specific training is needed in the repair of new products, FGI will provide such training. ¶ It is a pleasure to have G.E. Electronics as a member of our FGI family. We are looking forward to many years of cooperation between our two companies.

JOB 4 • Block Letter: Service Center Purpose and Procedures 23

JOB 4

ENRICHMENT ACTIVITY

REVIEW OF SERVICE CENTER PROCEDURES

SUPPLIES
This Page.

INSTRUCTIONS
Without referring to the letter which you just keyed to Señor Estrella, answer these questions about FGI's Service Center Purpose and Procedures.

1. What is the structure of the Service Center in Mexico?

   _____ Set up as an FGI Office

   _____ Set up in an existing Mexican electronics company.

2. All parts used in the repair of FGI electronic toys and games must be real FGI parts. Are there any exceptions to this policy? _____

3. If the Service Center repair person thinks a product can be repaired if the original circuitry is modified slightly, can he or she do that without approval from FGI?

   _____ Yes _____ No

   Why would such a procedure be in FGI's best interests? _____

   _____

4. Since Service Centers are responsible for repairs only, should they be concerned if an FGI product does not meet consumer safety requirements in the countries in which they are located? _____ Yes _____ No

   Why?_____

   _____

5. Instead of setting up a Service Center in Mexico, why doesn't FGI just include a statement with its Warranty telling customers to send defective products back to the manufacturer? _____

   _____

   _____

JOB 4 • Enrichment Activity

6. What is the name of a Service Center in your area that would repair the following products?

   Product   **Service Center in Your Area**

   a. Nikon Camera   _____

                              _____

   b. Braun Shaver   _____

                              _____

   c. BMW   _____

                              _____

   d. GE Refrigerator   _____

                              _____

TWO-PAGE REPORT: LATIN AMERICAN CULTURE

SUPPLIES
Plain Paper

REFERENCE MANUAL
Report Format (Note format for page 2.)
Proofreader's Marks

INSTRUCTIONS
Rekey report, making changes as indicated.

Single-space paragraph copy to keep report to two pages.

Be sure to check spelling. Spelling errors are not marked.

Customs and Manners in Latin America

An Orientation for FGI Personnel

As you travel and work in Latin American countries (Argentina, Belize, Bolivia, Brazil, Chile, Columbia, Costa Rica, Ecuador, Guatemala, Mexico, Panama, Paraguay, Peru, Uruguay, Venezuela), we offer this guide to help you deal correctly with people and to respect the way things are done in Latin America and to save you time in adapting your behavior from our culture to theirs.

Greetings

Most people in Latin American countries shake hands; sometimes they kiss on the cheek, or embrace. Titles are very important and should be used with people's names; therefore, when you are introduced, be sure to use an appropriate courtesy or professional title with the person's name. Also, people use the family names of both parents in their surnames; the mother's name is first. For example, Rosa Diaz Rodriguez would be greeted as "Señorita Diaz Rodriguez" or more informally as "Señorita Diaz."

Conversation

Latin Americans are very tactful and diplomatic. In both speaking and writing, Latin Americans tend to be indirect, elaborate, and very complimentary. They stand close to one another when they talk; if you back away, they might think you are snobbish or aloof. To make a good impression, you will want to learn something about the country you're visiting. For example, you might want to learn something about soccer. Soccer is a major sport in most Latin American countries. And remember that Latin Americans consider themselves Americans; they might resent people from the U.S. using "Americans" solely for United States citizens. One other point about conversation: Do not be insulted if someone calls you a "gringo." The word is not necessarily negative. In Peru, for example, "gringo" describes a blond, fair-skinned person.

Language

The official languages of a Latin American country is either Spanish or Portuguese. Even if business is conducted in English, learn some key phrases in the

FYI

ENGLISH

English is spoken daily by more than 750 million people. It is universally used for air-traffic control, scholarship, science, computer databases, international diplomacy and commerce. Of the 750 million who use English regularly, only about 300 million are native speakers—born in Great Britain, Canada, the U.S., Australia, New Zealand, and parts of South Africa and South America. English is studied and used worldwide because of the popularity of some elements of American culture, such as movies and music.

---

official language of the country. This effort shows recognition of and respect for the language of the culture.

Dress

One of the easiest ways to offend is to dress inappropriately. Dress that is too casual or too revealing is very offensive in many Latin American countries. To be safe, you should dress conservatively. Men should wear suits; women, suits or dresses.

Business Practices

You need a contact to get you an first meeting with someone. When you meet the person, you are expected to establish a personel relationship before getting down to business. So be sure you know something about the culture and area.

Business hours very from country to country. In many countries, businesses are open from 9 a.m. to 5 p.m. Monday through Friday. In other countries they are open from 9 a.m. to noon and from 2 or 2:30 p.m. to 6 p.m.

If you receive a letter in Spanish or Portugese, be sure to answer it in Spanish or Portguese. And remember these cultural differences: (1) the metric system is used for size or weight specifciations; (2) Latin Americans write dates in European style--first the day, then the month, and then the year (9/12/40 would be December 9, 1940); (3) in some countries, when people write out sums of money, periods distinguish thousands and commas denote fractions (C$5.000,50 is 5,000 Chilean pesos and 50 cents); and (4) the hours of the day are written on the basis of a 24-hour day--not two 12-hour periods (2 a.m. is 0200, 2 p.m. is 1400).

Meals

In Spanish-speaking Latin American countries, breakfast is "el desayuno" (el deh-sah-yoo-noh), lunch is "el almuerzo" (el ahl-mwehr-soh), and dinner is "la cena" (lah seh-nah) or "la comida" (lah koh-mee-dah). In generla, Latin Americans eat in the continental style--with the knife in the right hand and the fork in the left, using the knife to push food onto the back of the fork. Do not observe the United States custom of keeping the left hand on the lap as you eat; keep both hands above the table.

In most places, avoid raw vegetables, unpeeled fruit, and raw shellfish. Drink only bottled water, and don't drink fruit juices made with tap water. Don't use ice cubes made with tap water. Always ask for drinks *sin hielo* (seen yeh-loh), without ice.

Transportation

Use public transportation (taxis, subways, and buses). In most Latin American countries, it is best not to drive. Traffic is extremely congested, and in many countries the drivers pay little attention to driving rules.

JOB 5

ENRICHMENT ACTIVITY

CULTURAL DIVERSITY

SUPPLIES
This Page
TV Listings

INSTRUCTIONS
Watch TV over a five-day period.

Identify TV personalities in the news or entertainment programs who are representative of specific cultural heritages.

CULTURAL REPRESENTATION IN TELEVISION PROGRAMMING

Program Name	Cultural Diversity Factors Character Name	Cultural Representation
CBS News	Connie Chung	Asian news broadcaster

JOB 5 • Enrichment Activity 31

JOB 6

TABLE: ORDER/SHIPPING PROCESS FOR MEXICO

SUPPLIES
Plain Paper

REFERENCE MANUAL
Table Format
Proofreader's Marks

INSTRUCTIONS
Key the following in a table format.

Use a 1 1/2" top and 1" side or default margins.

Title table **Order/Shipment Processing Sequence.**

Determine spaces between columns.

Check spelling; errors have not been marked.

FYI

INTERNATIONAL WORDS

airport	fax
hello	hotel
bank	salad
bus	sport
camera	menu
doctor	dollar
Miss	Mister
telephone	okay
computer	police

FUNCTION	FGI STEPS	MEXICAN REPRESENTATIVE
Order writing	Determine availability. Notify representative. Submit order.	Determine product. Establish payment terms. Submit Order.
Order editing	Verify order.	Verify order. Notify customer of product availability.
Order approval	Enter using LOTUS. Produce hard copy. FAX copy to representative.	Verify order.
Credit check	Verify customer credit through credit department. Notify representative.	Clarify questions concerning customer credit.
Order mgmt.	Enter hard copy info onto log of history of account--receipt of order thru payment.	
Order entry	Enter into mainframe.	
Order shipment	FAX bill of lading, shipping records, and packing lists.	Coordinate shipment and correct documentation.
Billing	Create/send customer invoice.	Receives FAX of invoice.
Follow-up	Confirm receit of shipment.	Receives FAX of shipment.
Collection	Send monthly statement. Log remittances. Check past-due accounts and pursue collection.	Pursue collection.

JOB 6

ENRICHMENT ACTIVITY

A MATTER OF ETHICS

SUPPLIES
This Page

INSTRUCTIONS
Read the definition of "ethics."

Read the seven situations; using what is considered ethical (right or wrong) behavior in the United States, answer the question(s) for each situation.

Ethics is a system of right and wrong conduct in a particular culture. What might be ethical (lawful or accepted practice) in one culture might not be ethical in another culture. For example, in Mexico, it is expected that you give a government official some money to have the official speed up processing procedures. In the United States that would be called a bribe, and it is illegal.

1. You have a password that lets you use the computers here at school. Only students who have paid a fee and who are enrolled in a computer class are allowed access to the computers. A friend wants to borrow your password so he can use the computer for one of his projects. Is it ethical for you to lend your password to someone else?

    Answer _____ . Why? _____

    _____

    _____

    _____

2. A copy of WordPerfect 5.1 software is kept in your word processing lab. It is copyrighted; your school has permission to install it on the computers in the lab. You want to install the software on your computer at home. Is it ethical for you to install the software on your computer?

    Answer _____ . Why? _____

    _____

    _____

    _____

    _____

    _____

3. You have a friend who is really good with computers. She is really a "computer hacker"—a person who works and plays around with computers so much that she can do just about anything with them. She tells you that she can get into the database at school and change some of your grades in courses that you've taken; she assures you that the changes will never be detected. Even if you feel the changes won't be detected, is it ethical for you to ask her to do it?

   Answer _____ . Why? _____

   _____

   _____

   _____

   _____

4. You are driving a car in which you and a friend from Mexico are riding. You get stopped for speeding in your home town. When the police officer asks you for your license, you hand over your license and your friend extends his hand to give the officer a $10 bill.

   What would you do? _____

   _____

   _____

   _____

   _____

   What would you say to your friend? _____

   _____

   _____

   _____

   _____

5. The laws in the United States make it illegal for a United States company to use bribes to influence business decision making in other countries. If you are doing business in a country where a bribe is expected, as a United States businessperson, what would you do? Why? _____

   _____

   _____

6. A friend from Brazil asks you to bring some fruit to some people back in the states. The Department of Agriculture enforces the law that forbids a person to bring fruit from other countries into the United States. When you enter the United States from another country, you have to list items from other countries that you are bringing into the United States. Sometimes you are asked to show everything as well as list it. Your friend suggests that you just put it in your suitcase and no one will know about it when you enter this country.

   Would you do it? _____ Yes _____ No Explain _____

   _____

   _____

   _____

   _____

   _____

7. You have a friend from Costa Rica who has a visa to work here. Your friend asks you if he has to be absolutely accurate in reporting his income and expenses to the Internal Revenue Service for income tax purposes. He can't believe the IRS would ever know the difference. What would you tell him?

   _____

   _____

   _____

   _____

JOB 7

MEMO WITH REFERENCE SHEET: EXPORT EFFORTS AND MISTAKES

SUPPLIES

Eight Sheets Plain Paper

REFERENCE MANUAL

Organizational Chart for FGI

Formal Memo Format

Proofreader's Marks

INSTRUCTIONS

Key the following memo.

Send it to each of the four managers in our International Sales Division.

Select and key the wording of the subject line.

Key and attach the one-page report, "Ten Common Mistakes in Exporting," using single spacing with double spacing between numbered items.

Be sure to include the Attachment notation at end of each memo after your initials.

Check spelling.

Our exporting eforts have been fairly succesful in the last ten years. As we consider new international markets, I've studied our track record amd talked to the U. S. Department of Commerce.

Here is a summary of what seem to be the ten most common mistakes made by exporters. This summary is atached. Please review it with your people and use it as a reminder of key points as you maintain present markets and make plans to enter new ones.

TEN COMMON MISTAKES IN EXPORTING

1. Failure to define clearly the goals and objectives and to develope a written plan to acomplish them.

   Remember: Considerable help is available from such sources as the U. S. Department of Commerce, commercial banks, and our own state's Department of Commerce.

2. Failure to select carefuly the overseas distributors.

   Remember: It is difficult to protect our patents and trade marks in another country.

3. Failure to train and support international distributors.

   Remember: Train and assist international distributors so they can activly promote there accounts.

4. Failure to treat international distributors on an equal basis with domestec distributors.

   Remember: Give international distributors the same support that is provided for domestic distributors—advertising campaigns, special discount offers, warranty offers, etc.

5. Failure to consider unique market techniques in certain markets.

   Remember: What works in one market may not work in another!

6. Failure to modify product to meet regulations or cultural preferrences of other countries.

   Remember: Local safety and security codes, import restrictions, and cultural preferences cannot be ignored.

(Continued on next page)

JOB 7 • Memo with Reference Sheet: Export Efforts and Mistakes 37

FYI

THE EUROPEAN COMMUNITY

The European Community (EC) is a group of European countries that have signed a trade agreement to promote the free movement of goods, services, money, and labor among members. The members have standardized their trade rules, taxes, and health and safety standards. Trademarks and patents are honored throughout the EC.

7. Failure to print service, sale, and warrenty messages in locally-understood languages.

8. Failure to consider using an export managment company.

    Remember: Complexities of some markets justify this use.

9. Failure to consider licensing or joint-venture agreements.

10. Failure to provide servicing for products.

JOB 7

ENRICHMENT ACTIVITY

LANGUAGE AND PROOFREADING SKILLS (SWAHILI—A TRADE LANGUAGE)

SUPPLIES
This Page

REFERENCE MANUAL
Proofreader's Marks

INSTRUCTIONS
Test your skill in using correct grammar and punctuation by marking needed corrections in the following cultural reference information.

Use proofreader's marks to show what corrections are to be made.

SWAHILI--A TRADE LANGUAGE

Swahili began as a trade language on the East Coast of africa. It is used through out southeast and central Africa in such countries as Kenya Tanzania Zaire and Uganda. It is estimated that some 45 million people speak Swahili as their native language.

Swahili words is easy to pronounce. The vowels a, e, i, o, and u are pronounced "ah", "eh", "ee", "oh," and "oo". In a two- syllable word, you stress the first syllable. For example, **Tena** is pronounced TEH-na and means again. In a longer word, you stress the next-to-the-last syllable. For example, good-bye is **Kwaheri** (pronounced kwa-HEH-ree).

Since many independent African nations was once british colonies some Swahili words are used by people who speak english. For example, **bwana** and **safari**. Bwana of course means "master" safari means "trip."

The fact that some african nations was british colonies account for the Swahili words that are based on English words. **Hoteli** is based on the word "hotel." **Baa** comes from the English word "bar", **siteki** comes from the English word "steak". Other Swahili words that are based on English words is as follows **dansi** (dance), **karati** (carrots), **keki** (cake), **motokari** (car), **tiketi** (ticket), **petroli** (gasoline), and **jipi** (jeep).

(Continued on next page)

JOB 7 • Enrichment Activity 39

Swahilis simple pronunciation is a major reason for it's increasing use through southeast and central Africa. It is a language that is on its way to becoming a important world language.

Name: _____ Date: _____

PERFORMANCE REVIEW

WORK TRAITS RATING SCALE

Directions: Under each listed trait, circle the rating that applies to the student/worker named above for work through Job 7.

Organization: Consider arrangement of work area, use of references, handling of materials, etc.

0   Disorganized
1   Occasionally disorganized
2   Usually organized
3   Organized

Time Use: Consider task orientation, amount of supervision required, etc.

0   Inattentive; needs frequent supervision; wastes time.
1   Occasionally inattentive; needs routine supervision.
2   Generally attentive; follows directions independently.
3   Attentive; needs little supervision; is conscientious.

Instructions: Consider ability to understand, retain, and carry out written and oral instructions.

0   Rarely follows directions; asks many questions; requires repeated instruction.
1   Follows directions adequately; some additional instruction needed.
2   Follows directions adequately.
3   Follows directions with above-average problem-solving skills.

Reaction to Feedback: Consider immediate and long-term reaction to constructive criticism.

0   Hostile.
1   Indifferent.
2   Generally receptive.
3   Responsive; uses feedback to improve performance.

_____   Total points

Performance Review

Name: _____ Date: _____

PRODUCTION PROBLEM RATING GUIDE

Production Item	Factors to Be Evaluated	AL	AF	RATINGS* Problems 1 2 3 4 5 6 7
Letters	1. Letter style 2. Punctuation style 3. Vertical placement 4. Horizontal placement 5. Accuracy of copy 6. Corrections neatly made 7. Special lines properly placed 8. Envelope addresses			
Tables	1. Vertical placement 2. Horizontal placement 3. Spacing above/below heading 4. Spacing above/below secondary heading 5. Placement of column headings 6. Accuracy of copy 7. Corrections neatly made			
Reports	1. Appropriate top/bottom margins 2. Appropriate side margins 3. Headings appropriately placed 4. Correct spacing above/below headings 5. Correct spacing of body material 6. Accuracy of copy 7. Corrections neatly made 8. Division of words			
Application Form	1. Alignment with headings 2. Alignment of type on lines 3. Position of type in relation to vertical lines 4. Accuracy of copy 5. Corrections neatly made 6. Division of words			

Rating Scale: * A = Acceptable   NA = Not Acceptable

JOB 8
TWO-PAGE REPORT: AFRICAN CULTURE

SUPPLIES
Two Pages Plain Paper

REFERENCE MANUAL
Report Format
Proofreader's Marks

INSTRUCTIONS
Key the cultural information report single-spaced to keep it to two pages.

FYI

PROHIBITED ITEMS

The U.S. Customs Regulations will not allow you to bring the following items into the U.S.:

Illegal drugs, narcotics, toxic substances, liquor-filled candy. Agricultural products that might injure U.S. crops. Endangered species and their by-products (for example, tortoise-shell comb). Obscene publications.

Customs and Manners in Africa
An Orientation for FGI Personnel

Africa is a large, diverse continent. It is divided into three major subdivisions: northern nations, middle nations, and Southern Africa. For protocol and etiquette, the northern nations follow muslim or arabic customs; the middle nations follow customs oriented to black multicultures, and south african follows tribal black African influences as well as some English customs.

Because of the diversity among the countries in Africa, only a few basic guidelines for protocol and etiquette are presented here. If you are going to spend some time in a particular country, please use aditional resources for more information.

Languages

For the 16 countries in West Africa and the eight countries in central africa, French is the official language for the majority East African Coast. In South Africa, the main languages are Afrikaan, English, Nguni, and Sotho. For North Africa, Arabic and French are the official languages of most of the countries. Swahili is the official language along the East African coast.

Punctuality

In most of the African countries, you are expected to be on time. In Algeria, Ghana, Morocco, and Senegal, punctuality may be somewhat relaxed; however, you cannot go wrong by being on time. Appointments are recommended for business meetings.

Greetings

In addressing a person by name, use a professional title with the last name. It is common to shake hands when you greet someone or are introduced to a person. In some countries, the people also shake hands as they leave a person. So if a person extends a hand to you as you are about to leave, extend your hand to complete the handshake. In addition to the handshake, good friends--both men and women--may also kiss each other on the cheek.

Gifts

It is a custom to exchange small, inexpensive gifts during a business visit. Be prepared with a gift and follow the lead of the person with whom you are dealing. For example, in Algeria, gifts are normally exchanged during your second visit. In Zambia, do not give a gift to any government official.

(Continued on next page)

Conversational Topics

In many African countries, friendship and trust come before any business relationships. Good topics for friendly discussion are history, antiquity, culture, achievements, sports figures, religion, wildlife, national resources, arts, and world affairs. Stay away from such topics as politics and government leaders, inefficiency in local industries, military occupation by another country, or regional disputes, and racial unrest.

Gestures

Because there are so many different nationalities in Africa, it is hard to give do's and don'ts for gestures and body language. Once you are in an African country, you need to observe carefully what gestures and body language are appropriate. As a start, here are a few guidelines.

In an Arabic country or in a country where the Muslim religion is followed, sit properly without slouching or putting your feet on a table. Do not lean against a wall or put your hands in your pockets because both are considered disrespectful. Do not show the sole of your shoe or point it at someone; the soles are the lowest and dirtiest part of the body. And remember that the right hand is the prominent hand--use it to present gifts, gesture, touch, and eat. The left hand is generally regarded as the unclean hand and is used primarily for hygiene. And in many of these countries, women have traditionaly been considered inferior to men; they may not have direct eye contact with men or shake hands with them.

Money

Every country has its own currency. In West African countries, the Communaute Financielle Africaine (CFA) is the principal currency. In Kenya, the currency is the Kenya shilling; in Tanzania, it is the Tanzania shilling. Check with a local United States bank for the appropriate currency for the countries in which you will be travelling.

Africans are not in the habit of tipping, but as they move up the economic ladder, a small amount is expected. Everyone is expected to tip 10 percent at better restaurants. For taxis, travellers are expected to tip 10 percent.

Food

Quality of food varies greatly across Africa. In rural areas, you may eat local style (with your hands). African food typically consists of a staple like rice with some kind of sauce. The sauces have many spieces, most of which you can get only in Africa. Always wash your hands before you eat, and remember to use only your right hand in eating.

JOB 8

ENRICHMENT ACTIVITY

CURRENCY EXCHANGE RATES

SUPPLIES NEEDED

Local Newspaper.
This Page.

INSTRUCTIONS

Read the information about the exchange of local money for money from another country.

Look in the financial section of a newspaper from a large city to find the international exchange rates for the currencies listed here.

Use the published rates to figure how much foreign currency you would get for the dollar amounts shown in the chart.

For example, if the British exchange rate is 1.52 pounds for each U.S. dollar, $5 would equal $7.60 pounds (5.00 × 1.52).

When people travel internationally, they must change their money to the money of the country in which they are traveling. Rates of exchange for foreign currency for each United States dollar are published in the newspapers and are available from local banks and International Currency Exchange Offices.

INTERNATIONAL CURRENCY CONVERSIONS

International Currency	$1	$20.30	$45	$60.75	$100
Australia (Dollar)	_____	_____	_____	_____	_____
Britain (Pound)	_____	_____	_____	_____	_____
Belgium (Franc)	_____	_____	_____	_____	_____
Canada (Dollar)	_____	_____	_____	_____	_____
France (Franc)	_____	_____	_____	_____	_____
Germany (Mark)	_____	_____	_____	_____	_____
Greece (Drachma)	_____	_____	_____	_____	_____
Hong Kong (Dollar)	_____	_____	_____	_____	_____
Italy (Lira)	_____	_____	_____	_____	_____
Ireland (Punt)	_____	_____	_____	_____	_____
Japan (Yen)	_____	_____	_____	_____	_____
Kenya (Shilling)	_____	_____	_____	_____	_____
Mexico (Peso)	_____	_____	_____	_____	_____
Pakistan (Rupee)	_____	_____	_____	_____	_____
South Africa (Rand)	_____	_____	_____	_____	_____

JOB 8 • Enrichment Activity

International Currency	Dollar Amounts				
	$1	$20.30	$45	$60.75	$100
Spain (Peseta)	_____	_____	_____	_____	_____
Switzerland (Franc)	_____	_____	_____	_____	_____

1. In which country do you get the most for the U.S. dollar?

   _____

2. For which countries were the rates the hardest to calculate?

   _____

   _____

3. If you were traveling among several countries, how could you make it easy to know quickly how much a local price is in U.S. dollars?

   _____

   _____

   _____

   _____

   _____

JOB 9

LETTER WITH TABLE: ORDER CONFIRMATION

SUPPLIES
Two Sheets Plain Paper or Letterhead

Two Envelopes

REFERENCE MANUAL
Letter Format

INSTRUCTIONS
Key letter with a copy going to Washington Dean.

Decide number of spaces to leave between columns in table.

Check punctuation, spelling, and all figures.

Mr. Chinua Achebe
Director of Purchases
Quintesseme
Falomo Shopping Centre
Victoria Island
Nigeria

Dear Mr. Achebe

It was a pleasure to talk with you today. It was good to hear your voice and to learn that your fmaily is well.

Before we fill your order, would you please confirm that our records agree with your records for the quantitees desired and the amount due.

```
                                    Cost of Each
Item                       Qty.     in U. S.Dollars        Total

3901 The Silencer           75         11.50               862.50
2200 Girder Master          50          6.99               359.50
1014 Jammin                100          8.65               865.00
4480 Phase Blaster          85          9.99               894.15
1065 Midle East Magic      110          5.99               658.90

Total                                                    $3,640.05
```

Mr. Achebe when we receive your FAX, we will submit the order and sendan invoice too you. As we discussed, the full amount will be due within 30 days of the reciept of the toys.

Thank you for your business.

Sincerely yours

James Story, Director
International Sales
xxx

JOB 9

ENRICHMENT ACTIVITY

ETHNIC FOODS IN THE UNITED STATES

SUPPLIES

This Page

INSTRUCTIONS

Think about the different cultural foods that are available in the United States.

In the columns, list at least three examples of ethnic foods from the listed cultures. (For ideas, use local restaurants, travel books in the library, and/or talk to people.)

Country	Food Name	Food Description
Africa	Pan Fried Grubs	Snack—Grub Worms
	Chichinga	Meat Dish—Skewered Goat
	Yam Balls	Vegetable—Sweet Potatoes
	Jollof Rice	Meat Dish—Rice with Meat
China		
Mexico		
Greece		
Germany		

JOB 9 • Enrichment Activity

India   _____   _____

         _____   _____

         _____   _____

         _____   _____

Italy   _____   _____

         _____   _____

         _____   _____

         _____   _____

JOB 10: TABLE AND ONE-PAGE REPORT: TRAVEL ASSISTANCE

SUPPLIES
Two Plain Sheets of Paper

REFERENCE MANUAL
Long Table Format

Report Format

INSTRUCTIONS
Key Item 1 as a one-page long table.

Use 1" top and side margins.

Decide spaces between columns.

Key the topics in the left column in alphabetical order.

Key Item 2 as a single-spaced report.

Use 1" top and side margins.

Key the side headings in alphabetical order.

Run a spell check on Item 2; if you use spell check software, remember a spell checker may not find all errors.

ITEM 1

BUSINESS TRAVEL RESOURCES

Passport Information or Lost Passport	Office of Passport Services U. S. Department of State 1425 K Street NW Washington, DC 20520 (202-647-0518) (List name of local U.S. Post Office that provides the forms/information)
Identification & Location of U. S. Ambassadors	U. S. Department of State Washington, DC 20520 (202-647-6575)
Commerical Business/Trade Attaches; General Trade Information	U. S. Foreign & Commercial Svc. U. S. Department of Commerce Washington, DC 20230 (800-USA-TRADE)
International Driver's License	AAA (Supply nearest local office address & phone number)
Counsel for Release of Jailed Americans	International Legal Defense Counsel 111 South 15th Street Packard Bldg., 24th Floor Philadelphia, PA 19102 (215-077-9982)
Identification of English-Speaking Physicians in 140 Countries	International Association of Medical Assistance for Travelers 736 Center Street, Dept. TH Lewiston, NY 14092 (716-754-4883)
Traveler's Advisory	Citizen's Emergency Center Department of State (202-647-5225)
Vaccination Information	Center for Disease Control Atlanta, GA 30333 (404-639-1610)

FYI

PASSPORT OR VISA?

Passports are issued by the U.S. Department of State to citizens of the U.S. to identify them as Americans and to provide documentation to allow them to leave and reenter the U.S.
A visa is an official authorization that permits entry into and travel within a particular country for a specified period of time for a specific purpose. For example, visas are issued for business, study, or tourism.

Visa Services

Visa Services
1519 Connecticut Avenue, NW
Suite 300
Washington, DC 20036
(800-222-VISA)

Safety Advice
(Free Publication)

"A Safe Trip Abroad"
Superintendent of Documents
Washington, DC 20402

ITEM 2

SECURITY PROCEDURES

<u>Itinerary & Emergency Communication Plans</u>
Keep the following items in your office files while you are traveling:
    A copy of your itinerary, airline ticket, and passport
    A record of your blood type and Rh factor
    A list of any specific health conditions
    A copy of your eye glass prescription
    A photocopy of your traveler's check numbers
    A copy of your credit card numbers
    A list of key words or a code that can be used in case you are kidnaped and allowed to speak or write to outsiders.
    A list of people (with addresses and telephone numbers) to contact in case of emergency.

<u>Traveler's Checks</u>
Keep good records of your check numbers—one in the office and one with you. Enclude the telephone number needed to report loss or stolen checks.

<u>Hotel Security</u>
Remember that large first-class hotels where Americans and foreign executives are known to stay might be a terrorist target.

Do not carry any unecessary valuables with you—for example, jewelry or large amounts of cash.

Make hotel reservations in your own name and register your office address without the name of the company.

Request a room on the second or third floor in hotels in countries where fire safety is not given high priority. Upon checking into the hotel, review escape procedures in case of frie or other emergencies.

Before going to bed, place coat or other covering and valuables within easy reach for a quick escape.

<u>Auto Security</u>
Keep car windows closed and car doors locked while stopped at a light; also leave at least one car length between your car and the one in front of you.

Do not stop for acidents you see on the road.

Always lock your unattended car and conceel luggage and cameras.

JOB 10 • Table and One-Page Report: Travel Assistance

JOB 10

ENRICHMENT ACTIVITY

GEOGRAPHY REVIEW

SUPPLIES

Map on Page 53

INSTRUCTIONS

Identify the appropriate continent for each of the six numbers located on the map— Africa, Asia, Australia, Europe, North America, South America.

Using the countries listed here, place the letter of each country in its appropriate country outline on the map.

LISTED COUNTRIES

A.	China	B.	Brazil
C.	Canada	D.	Spain
E.	Portugal	F.	France
G.	Germany	H.	United States
I.	Venezuela	J.	Egypt
K.	Libya	L.	Chad
M.	Mexico	N.	Peru
O.	Ethiopia	P.	Kenya
Q.	Colombia	R.	India
S.	Poland	T.	Ireland
U.	Argentina	V.	Taiwan
W.	Saudi Arabia	X.	United Kingdom
Y.	Turkey	Z.	Pakistan

52   JOB 10 • Enrichment Activity

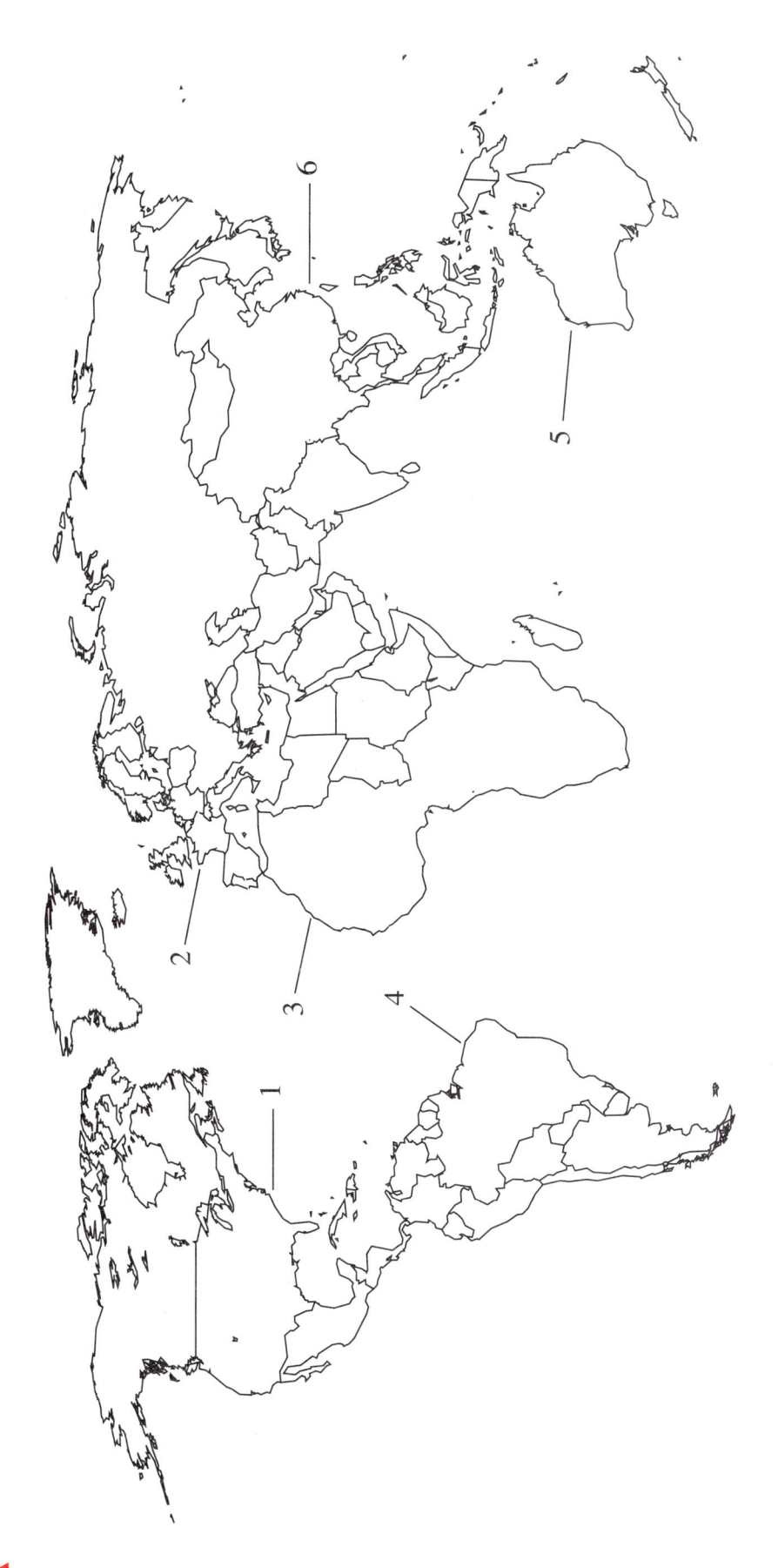

CONTINENTS AND COUNTRIES—WHAT IS WHERE?

JOB 10 • Enrichment Activity

53

JOB 11: FORM LETTERS: SERVICE CENTERS AND ACCOUNTS PAYABLE

SUPPLIES
8 Letterheads or Plain Paper
8 Envelopes

REFERENCE MANUAL
Letter Format

INSTRUCTIONS
Key the form letters.

Leave space for date, inside address, and salutation.

Use James Story's name and title on all letters.

Have your teacher review your keyed form letters.

After your form letters have been reviewed by your teacher, fill in each letter with the information that follows Form Letter 2.

FORM LETTER NO. 1: LOCATION OF SERVICE CENTERS

Your request for service of Fun & Games International products should be directed to the following FGI Service Center:

(Center Address Here)

This center's staff can handle repairs and replacement requests. They can also provide additional information about FGI products.

Thank you for your inquiry. It is a pleasure for us to provide this information.

Sincerely yours

FORM LETTER NO. 2: ACCOUNTS PAYABLE

Below is a listing of your account, reflecting only that portion which is overdue:

Invoice No.	Days Overdue	Amount Due in U.S. Dollars

If there are any questions concerning the amount owed, please FAX or call me. Otherwise, please send your payment within five days.

Your prompt attention to this matter will be appreciated.

Sincerely yours

QUALITY OF LIFE WORLDWIDE

INTERNATIONAL LIVING's 1993 Quality of Life Survey rated over 188 countries on cost of living, economic prosperity, recreation and cultural entertainment, infrastructure, health, freedom, and environment.

Top 5 Countries
United States
Canada
Switzerland
New Zealand
Norway

Bottom 5 Countries
Ethiopia
Zaire
Somalia
Chad
Burkina Faso

SERVICE CENTER INFORMATION REQUESTS

Inside Addresses	**Service Center Location**
Monsieur Andr Cresson 2 rue du Dome 75116 Paris France	FDP 122 rue Nollet 75017 Paris France
Mrs. Charlotte Cosgrove P. O. Box 96 Montreal, Quebec H4A 3L7 Canada	Monenco Electronics 40 Frontenac, Box 304 Montreal, Quebec H5A 1B4 Canada
Mr. Shawn O'Donnel Aras Failte Eyre Square, Galway Ireland	Paddy's Electronic Shop 4 Leeson Lane, Galway Ireland
Miss Hazel Williams Rosenbery Avenue London EC1 England	Schonberg's Repair Centre 17 Wilton Road London SW1 England

ACCOUNTS PAYABLE FORM LETTERS

Account	Invoice No.	Days Overdue	Amount Due in U.S. Dollars
Mr. Rasi Sayam Fatima Toy & Game Center 69 Soi Watana Sukhumvit Road, Bangkok Thailand	60043	45	$980.04
Ms. Stella Ting Toomey China National Electronics Import Corporation 49 Fuxing Road Beijing China	57603	60	$1,577.10

JOB 11 • Form Letters: Service Centers and Accounts Payable

Account	Invoice No.	Days Overdue	Amount Due in U.S. Dollars
Mr. Lawrence Holmes Windsor Puzzles & Games 64 St. James Street London SW1 England	00144	30	$2,250.00
Mr. Jaromir Malek Mamelouk 4 A Hassan Assem Street Cairo Egypt	10060	45	$860.55

JOB 11

ENRICHMENT ACTIVITY

SLANG EXPRESSIONS

A

SUPPLIES
This Page

INSTRUCTIONS
Remember to use simple, clear English expressions when you speak, write, or FAX information to people who have English as a second language.

Listed here are slang expressions used in the United States. For each expression, list a simple or clear way to say what you mean.

At the end of the list, add five of your own slang expressions and your simplification of what they mean.

U.S. Slang Word/Phrase	Simplified Expression
add fuel to the flame	make worse
behind the eight ball	in trouble; in a difficult position
bottom line	
on pins and needles	
on the ball	
hard nut to crack	
hard-nosed	
get the ax	
middle of the road	
make the grade	
freak out	

JOB 11 • Enrichment Activity 57

fit as a fiddle

wear the pants

weed out

give up the ship

by hook or by crook

feather in one's cap

fish out of water

have rocks in one's head

in a nutshell

JOB 12
THREE-PAGE REPORT: JAPANESE CULTURE

SUPPLIES
Three Sheets of Plain Paper

REFERENCE MANUAL
Report Format
Proofreader's Marks

INSTRUCTIONS
Key this information in a single-spaced report. Double-space between enumerated items.

Use 1" top and side margins or default margins.

Title it **Understanding and Working with the Japanese**; use the subtitle **An Orientation for FGI Personnel**.

Check spelling and punctuation.

Business in Japan is as much about building relationships as it is about negotiating contracts. The Japanese are intensely loyal to existing suppliers—because they know and trust them. Your first step must be to build trust and friendliness. Knowing something about Japanese verbal and nonverbal practices will help develop and strengthen your relationships with the Japanese business world.

Language

Japanese is not an easy language to learn. Most Japanese who went to school after WWII have studied English for at least six years; many take four more years of English in their university work. For these reasons, we speak English in our work their. You can make it easier for the Japanese to understand your English if you will do just six things:

1. Use short sentences.
2. Avoid slang.
3. Talk slowly.
4. Write your statements to clarify your meaning.
5. Summarize frequently.
6. Offer to provide a translator if communication proves too difficult.

Greetings

Before you bow, introduce yourself by giving your name and a phrase like "It is a pleasure" or "I am pleased." For the bow, stand facing the other person—men with their hands by their sides and women with their hands clasped in front of them; and bow to an angle of about 45 degrees. While bowing, keep your eyes on the ground; eye contact indicates a lack of humility.

A business card is almost as important to the Japanese as a name. The card should have English on one side and Japanese on the other. It is presented with both hands, with the Japanese translation face up toward the person. Use a quality holder for your own business cards since they represent you. Business cards must be treated with respect. Place them in your card holder and put them in your jacket or briefcase. Never put a business card in your hip pocket!

(Continued on next page)

When you receive another's card, take it with your right hand, and bow again. You **must** look at the card before you put it in your card holder, even if you know the person; this shows respect for the person.

Conversation

Topics of interest include the family, the weather, sports (baseball, golf, and Sumo), and your impressions of Japan. As you make conversation, do not mention minority groups (Koreans or the outcasts of Japan called Burakumin).

Social and Business Rules

The Japanese pay a lot of attention to nonverbal communication--they truly believe that actions speak louder and more accurately than words! Please be aware of these social and business rules:

1. The Japanese try to maintain a blank face. Showing emotions is regarded as undisciplined or embarrassing. Direct eye contact is thought to be impolite.
2. The Japanese tend to need more personal space than Americans. You should stand a little further away from the person than you normally would. Physical contact is generally frowned upon—no back slapping, arm touching, etc.
3. The Japanese stand and sit with good posture--it is a sign of good breeding.
4. Pushing and shoving in crowds and a reluctance to form orderly lines are common.
5. The bow is the accepted form of greeting and farewell in Japan. Therefore, a weak handshake does not imply weakness.
6. The Japanese society does not encourage individualism. Both men and women should avoid loud colors and dress conservatively. Women have to be careful not to overwhelm Japanese businessmen; conservative dress with low heels would be appropriate.
7. Business women should not expect seats to be offered or doors to be opened since men precede women in everything. American men, therefore, should not insist on Japanese women accepting typical American courtesies.
8. Always make an appointment and be punctual for it.
9. It is a common practice to give a gift for courtesies extended. Wrap the gift in high-quality, pastel-colored paper (never plain white). Hand the gift with both hands and do not expect it to be opened in your presence. Also, if a gift is given to you, do not open it until you are alone.

(Continued on next page)

SUPERSTITIONS

Throughout Europe as well as in Brazil, you should not seat 13 people at the same table—natives believe that one of the diners will die. Nine is unlucky in Japan; it represents hard times or a struggle. Never set up a business meeting at 9 a.m. or a celebration on the 9th of a month. Eight is a lucky number in Hong Kong; it means prosperity. It is often found in phone numbers and addresses of Hong Kong establishments around the world. Restaurants even set prices to include the number 8.

10. Chopsticks are frequently used as eating utensils--practice the correct way to use them. Do not use just one or point to anyone or anything with them. Always place them on the chopsticks rest--not on your bowl.

JOB 12

ENRICHMENT ACTIVITY

CULTURAL REVIEW

INSTRUCTIONS

Without looking at the cultural notes that you keyed in Job 12, see how much information you can recall by answering these questions.

1. Why do the Japanese use English when working with FGI personnel?

    a. _____

    b. _____

2. In speaking English with the Japanese, give two suggestions for making it easier for them to understand you. (Students may list any of the following.)

    a. _____

    b. _____

    c. _____

    d. _____

    e. _____

    f. _____

3. Besides bowing, what do you do when you greet a Japanese businessperson?

    _____

    _____

    _____

4. Why do you avoid direct eye contact in introductions to Japanese businesspeople?

    _____

5. When you receive a business card from a Japanese businessperson, what four things should you do with it?

    a. _____

    b. _____

JOB 12 • Enrichment Activity 63

c. _____

d. _____

6. What is a good conversational topic in Japan? _____

_____

Think about nonverbal communication in Japan and identify the following statements as either True or False.

_____ 1. In talking to the Japanese, you should stand closer to them than you would to Americans.

_____ 2. The Japanese show a lot of emotion in their faces.

_____ 3. The Japanese do not give a lot of direct eye contact.

_____ 4. It is impolite to push and shove in crowds in Japan.

_____ 5. The Japanese society encourages individualism.

_____ 6. Businesswomen are shown courtesies in Japan just as they are in America—doors opened, seats offered.

_____ 7. If you receive a gift in Japan, open it immediately and express appreciation for it.

_____ 8. In eating, always place your chopsticks on your bowl when they are not being used.

_____ 9. Good posture in Japan is a sign of breeding.

_____ 10. American businesswomen should wear high heels in Japan so they can impress Japanese businessmen.

JOB 13

TWO TABLES: JAPANESE HOLIDAYS AND TOURIST ATTRACTIONS

SUPPLIES
Two Sheets of Plain Paper

REFERENCE MANUAL
Short Table Format
Long Table Format

INSTRUCTIONS

Key Table No. 1 in an attractive two-column format.

Use the title **Holidays in Japan;** use the subtitle **A Reference Guide for Travel and Business Planning.**

Use short table format guidelines.

Key Table No. 2 using long table format guidelines.

Begin the title **Sightseeing In/Near Tokyo** on line 7.

Use 1" side or default margins; decide spaces between columns.

Arrange the listings in each city in alphabetical order. Put the palaces in Kyoto in alphabetical order, too.

TABLE NO. 1

DATE	HOLIDAY
January 1	Gantan (New Year's Day)
January 15	Seijin-no-Hi (Adult's Day)
February 11	Kenkoku kinen-bi (National Foundation Day)
March 20	Shunbun-no-Hi (Spring Equinox)
April 29–May 5	Golden Week
April 29	Tenno Tanjobi (Birthday of the late Emperor Hirohito)
May 3	Kempa kinen-bi (Constitution Memorial Day)
May 5	Kodomo-no-Hi (Children's Day)
September 15	Keiro-no-Hi (Respect for the Aged Day)
September 23	Shubun-no-Hi (Autumn Equinox)
October 10	Taiiku-no-Hi (Health and Sports Day)
November 3	Bunka-no-Hi (Culture Day)
November 23	Kinro kansha-no-Hi (Labor Thanksgiving Day)
December 28–January 5	New Year Celebration

TABLE NO. 2

CITY	SIGHT
Tokyo	Imperial Palace—Emperor's Palace
	Tokyo National Museum
	Asakusa Kannon Temple
	Meiji Shrine
Kyoto	Palaces: Old Imperial Palace
	Katsura Imperial Villa
	Shugakuin Imperial Villa
	Heian Shrine
	Saihoji Temple
	Kyoto National Museum

FYI

TRANSLATION AND INTERPRETATION

Translating and interpreting are not the same thing! A translator converts written material in one language into written form in another language. An interpreter works only in spoken words.

<u>CITY</u>   <u>SIGHT</u>

Kamakura   Museum of National Treasures
           Shirahata Daimyojin
           Kamakura-Gu Shrine
           Sugimoto-Dera (Kamakura's Oldest Temple)
           Buddha Hall
           Zeniarai Benten
           Great Buddha of Kamakura

Nikko   Toshogu Shrine
           Nikko Museum
           Treasure House
           Nikko-Edo Mura (Feudal Village)

JOB 13

ENRICHMENT ACTIVITY

ETHNIC HOLIDAYS AND CELEBRATIONS IN THE UNITED STATES

INSTRUCTIONS

Test your knowledge of American national holidays by identifying the month in which each of these holidays occurs.

Holiday	Month/Day
New Year's Day	January 1
Columbus Day	
Martin Luther King, Jr., Day	
Independence Day	
Veterans' Day	
Presidents' Day	
Memorial Day	
Labor Day	
Thanksgiving Day	
Christmas	

INSTRUCTIONS

Think of the many ethnic and/or religious groups in the United States.

Identify one group and list its major holidays and/or celebrations; for example, Jewish, Greek Orthodox, American Indian, Muslim.

Use resources such as the library, your friends, relatives, clergy, etc.

Group	Holiday or Celebration	Month/Day	Purpose

Group	Holiday or Celebration	Month/Day	Purpose

JOB 14

TWO-PAGE MEMO: GREETINGS AND BUSINESS CARDS

SUPPLIES
Two Sheets of Paper

REFERENCE MANUAL
Formal Memo Format
Second-Page Heading Format
Proofreader's Marks

INSTRUCTIONS
Key this two-page memo.

Send it to Marketing Personnel.

Use the subject: Etiquette for Greetings and Business Cards.

Check spelling and punctuation.

As we do business in other countries and as we receive businesspeople from other countries ~~here~~ in our American offices, it is important to know how to great ~~people~~ /them and how to present our business cards. The greeting is the beginning of the business interaction; if it goes well, we create a positive impression ~~to~~ (that will) serve as a foundation for our business discussions.

Business Cards

The ultimate passport in today's global economy is the business card. It (identifies your company and) ~~proves that you exist, it~~ makes it easier for international people to understand your name, ~~and it gives your rank and profession.~~ Rank and profession in other countries are taken much more seriously than they are in the united states.

For every country in which you travel, have your business card information in English on one side and in the language of the particular country on the other side. Include your name, ~~your~~ position title, ~~and~~ your company name and address, and your FAX and telephone numbers.

In european and north american countries, the business card may be presented with either hand. In southeast Asia, Africa, and the middle East, never present the card with your left hand; the left hand is considered unclean. ~~In Japan, present your business card with both hands, and make sure the type is facing the recipient.~~

Greetings

Your first chance to make an impression is when you greet someone and exchange names. In America, we tend to be less formal but that does not mean we should be careless. Social and Professional family status are very important in ~~other~~ many cultures. If you say or do something which is incorrect, you can offend, and /others embarrass ~~people~~ /yourself.

Always use a formal greeting when you meet people from other cultures. Never address them by their first names unless they ask you to do so. In European and North American countries, greet the person with a firm handshake, good eye contact, and the pronunciation of the last name with a courtesy title--Mrs. Moschler.

In Latin American countries, greet a person with a light handshake and maybe an embrace. Remember that most peoples' names are a combination of the father's and mother's name. Only the mother's name is used in conversation. So, Carlos Mendoza-Zamora would be addressed as ~~Mr.~~ /Señor Mendoza.

JOB 14 • Two-Page Memo: Greetings and Business Cards 69

WORDS OF LOVE

Give the traditional Valentine's Day greeting an international accent with these global renditions of the words I love you.

French	Je t'aime
German	Ich liebe Dich
Italian	Ti amo
Spanish	Te amo
Swedish	Jag alskar dej
Dutch	Ik hou van je
Polish	Kocham cie
Romanian	Te iubesc

The French also greet one another with a light handshake; the firm U.S.-type handshake is thought to be impolite. Generally, women do not shake hands. Young people and close friends will frequently exchange kisses on both cheeks in addition to the handshake. And the French often shake hands in departing.

In the Orient, the Chinese system presents the surname first and the given name last; for example, Wang Xiansheng would be addressed as Mr. Wang. However, if the Chinese are using English, they will usually put their surname last as is done in the United States. When you greet Chinese people, shake hands and address them by their surname with a courtesy title.

For India and Thailand, a greeting consists of putting your hands together in a prayer-like position, holding them about chest high, and then bowing slightly. In India, this is called NAMASTE; in Thailand, it is called wai. People are addressed by their surname with the appropriate courtesy title.

In Muslim countries, people may greet each other with Assalaamualaikum (Peace be upon you) and Waalaikum assalaam (And peace be upon you). Men may shake hands; however, remember that you should not shake hands, kiss, or embrace a member of the opposite sex.

Homework

You can see how easy it could be to insult someone or embarrass yourself as you meet and greet people. Please do your homework before you travel. Prepare your business cards and study the customs. We want to build relationships based upon respect for and appreciation of other cultures.

JOB 14

ENRICHMENT ACTIVITY

FOREIGN LANGUAGE VOCABULARY

INSTRUCTIONS

Using such resources as your family, friends, students and faculty involved in foreign language courses, and foreign language reference books in the library and bookstores, write the Spanish vocabulary for these words and phrases. Also choose one other language and write the vocabulary of that language for the words and phrases.

Words/Phrases	Spanish Language	French Language
Good day	Buenos días	Bonjour
Good evening		
Hello		
Good-bye		
How are you?		
Very well		
My name		
Mr.		
Mrs.		
Miss		
Yes		
No		
Thank you		
You're welcome		
Please		
I don't understand		
Excuse me		
Slowly		

JOB 14 • Enrichment Activity 71

Words/Phrases	Spanish Language	French Language
What is this?	_____	_____
Right	_____	_____
Left	_____	_____
Do you speak English?	_____	_____

Name: _____ Date: _____

PERFORMANCE REVIEW

WORK TRAITS RATING SCALE

Directions: Under each listed trait, circle the rating that applies to the student/worker named above for work through Job 14.

Organization: Consider arrangement of work area, use of references, handling of materials, etc.

0 Disorganized
1 Occasionally disorganized
2 Usually organized
3 Organized

Time Use: Consider task orientation, amount of supervision required, etc.

0 Inattentive; needs frequent supervision; wastes time.
1 Occasionally inattentive; needs routine supervision.
2 Generally attentive; follows directions independently.
3 Attentive; needs little supervision; is conscientious.

Instructions: Consider ability to understand, retain, and carry out written and oral instructions.

0 Rarely follows directions; asks many questions; requires repeated instruction.
1 Follows directions adequately; some additional instruction needed.
2 Follows directions adequately.
3 Follows directions with above-average problem-solving skills.

Reaction to Feedback: Consider immediate and long-term reaction to constructive criticism.

0 Hostile.
1 Indifferent.
2 Generally receptive.
3 Responsive; uses feedback to improve performance.

_____ Total points

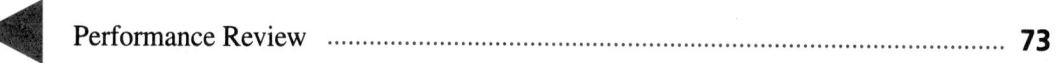

Name: _____   Date: _____

PRODUCTION PROBLEM RATING GUIDE

Production Item	Factors to be Evaluated	RATINGS* Problems 8 9 10 11 12 13 14
Letters	1. Letter style 2. Punctuation style 3. Vertical placement 4. Horizontal placement 5. Accuracy of copy 6. Corrections neatly made 7. Special lines properly placed 8. Envelope addresses	
Tables	1. Vertical placement 2. Horizontal placement 3. Spacing above/below heading 4. Spacing above below secondary heading 5. Placement of column headings 6. Accuracy of copy 7. Corrections neatly made	
Reports	1. Appropriate top/bottom margins 2. Appropriate side margins 3. Headings appropriately placed 4. Correct spacing above/below headings 5. Correct spacing of body material 6. Accuracy of copy 7. Corrections neatly made 8. Division of words	
Application Form	1. Alignment with headings 2. Alignment of type on lines 3. Position of type in relation to vertical lines 4. Accuracy of copy 5. Corrections neatly made 6. Division of words	

Rating Scale: * A = Acceptable   NA = Not Acceptable

REFERENCE MANUAL

The following pages provide instructions and models for the preparation of written communications. These guidelines are to be followed by all Fun & Games International employees.

Instruction	*Page*
FGI Organizational Chart	76
Proofreader's Marks	77
Formal Memorandum Format	78
Simplified Memorandum Format	79
Second-Page Memo Heading Format	80
Short Table Format Guides	81
Long Table Format Guides	82
Report Format Guides	83–84
Block-Style Letter Format	85
Envelope Formats	86
International Time Zones Chart	87
Domestic Time Zones Map	88

Organizational Chart
Sales and Customer Service

- **MARK WEBSTER** — C.E.O.
  - **BARBARA WEHIR** — President
    - **CHRIS HEWETT** — Admin. Asst.
    - **NEAL BULLA** — V.P. Marketing
      - **HELEN STROTHER** — Admin. Asst.
      - **JAQUETTA SEARLE** — Dir. Pkg. Dev. Merchandising
      - **DONNA ZALESKI** — Dir. Media.
    - **CLARENCE KUPPER** — V.P. Sales
      - **BETTY LOCKLEAR** — Admin. Asst.
      - **JAMES STORY** — Dir. Int. Sales
        - **JULIE RIGALLI** — Sales Mgr. Canada, Mexico
        - **NEENA PELLEGRINI** — Sales Mgr. Europe
        - **WASHINGTON DEAN** — Sales Mgr. Africa
        - **LUN KI CHAN** — Sales Mgr. Asia
      - **KYLE BROWN** — Dir. Domestic Sales
        - **VENEVA CATO** — Sales Mgr. East Coast
        - **MARYA ZUKE** — Sales Mgr. West Coast
        - **GORDON BENNING** — Sales Mgr. Central
        - **KEVIN DENNEDY** — Sales Mgr. Natl. Accts.
    - **HAZEL REID** — V.P. Finance
      - **ROBYN TUCCI** — Admin. Asst.
      - **LEROY RUSSEL** — Mgr. Computer
      - **HERB CRONSTEIN** — Mgr. Payroll
    - **ANTONIO VILLAS** — Dir. Sales Admin.
      - **JOHN METZGER** — Cust. Service
      - **PAULINE O'HARE** — Telemarketing

FUN INTERNATIONAL GAMES

76 — Introduction

PROOFREADER'S MARKS

Please use proofreader's marks to save time and communicate more clearly the changes that need to be made in documents.

Marks		Copy Example
∧	= insert	If the pakage includes...
⌒	= close up	...every thing included.
ϑ	= delete	The bodye is single-spaced.
ϑ̸	= delete/close up	This is alttered for now.
∼	= transpose	Do nto indent.
≡	= capitalize	it is also typed.
# or #⁄	= insert space	Don't open with "we."
∧⁄	= insert punctuation	Do not use a comma do use a colon.
sp	= spell out	sp ⑨ is not enough.
¶	= paragraph	It is typed in the left corner. ¶ If a letter is confidential, "Personal" is typed on the letter.
No new ¶	= no new paragraph	All external correspondence is in letter format, not memo format. No new ¶ The memo format is only used inside the company.
⊏	= move left	⊏ Double-space the body.
⊐	= move right	⊐ Single-space the address.
lc	= lowercase	Do not use a lc Title.
∥	= align/set flush	∥ It is also typed in the lower ∥ left corner of the envelope.
STET	= leave it as it was originally	Use a courtesy t̲i̲t̲l̲e̲ such as "Ms." STET
____	= italics or underscore	It was labeled c̲o̲n̲f̲i̲d̲e̲n̲t̲i̲a̲l̲.

Formal Memorandum Format

Use a full sheet of plain paper.
Use 1" margins.
Begin TO on line 10.
Omit personal titles (Miss, Mr., Mrs., Ms., Dr.)

Double-space between the headings and between paragraphs.
Single-space lines in paragraphs.

FUN INTERNATIONAL GAMES
425 Fourth Street
P.O. Box 2000
Cincinnati, OH 45202-2000
513•555•3452 / 513•555•6350 (fax)

```
TO:   Antonio Villas, Director, Sales Administration         line 10
                        DS
FROM: Larry Bittner, Manufacturing Engineering
                        DS
DATE: February 14, 19--
                        DS
SUBJECT: Puerto Rico Service Center
                        DS
Based on our discussion, I have prepared the attached report. This    SS
clears the way for CompuElectronics to serve as our repair center for
"defective" electronic games.
                        DS
Please call me if you have any comments or questions.
                        DS
bm
                        DS
Attachment
```

SIMPLIFIED MEMORANDUM

Use a full sheet of plain paper.
Use block format and 1" or default margins.
Begin date on line 10.
Omit the word **Subject** and key the subject line in all caps.

Double-space between all parts, except below date and the last paragraph—quadruple-space below the dateline and below the last paragraph.

```
February 14, 19--     line 10
                                    QS
Antonio Villas, Director, Sales Administration
                                    DS
PUERTO RICO SERVICE CENTER
                                    DS
Based on our discussion, I have prepared the attached report. This   SS
clears the way for CompuElectronics to serve as our repair center for
"defective" electronic games.
                                    DS
Please call me if you have any comments or questions.
                                    QS
Larry Bittner, Manufacturing Engineering
                                    DS
bm
                                    DS
Attachment
```

Simplified Memorandum

SECOND-PAGE MEMO HEADING FORMAT

Begin on line 7.
Single-space heading information.
Use block format.
Key **Memo to** with name of addressee.
Key the word **Page** with the appropriate number on the second line.

Key the current date on the third line.
Double-space after the heading information and continue the document.

```
Memo to Señor Rodriguez      line 7
Page 2
Current Date
                              DS
1"   Separately, we are awaiting your comments to our June 19 FAX regarding
     submission of copies of the bill of lading for the L/C.

     djs
```

SHORT TABLE FORMAT GUIDES

Start on line 10 for a short table.
Use 1" or default side margins.
Center the main heading in all caps.
Double-space between main and secondary headings.
Key the secondary heading in caps/lowercase.

Double-space between the secondary heading and column headings or the body if there are no column headings.
Block and underline column headings.
Double-space between column headings and the body.
Double-space table content.

```
            SELECTED NATIONAL ECONOMIES    line 10
                         DS
             Gross National Product (in millions)
                         DS
             Country           GNP
                         DS
             Finland           $129,823
             Indonesia          101,151
             South Africa        90,410
             Poland              64,480
             Greece              60,245
             Algeria             51,585
             Singapore           33,512
```

LONG TABLE FORMAT GUIDES

Use 1" top, side and bottom margins.
Center heading in all caps.
Double-space between main and secondary heading.
Key secondary heading in caps/lowercase.
Double-space between secondary heading and column headings or body if there are no column headings.

Block and underline column headings.
Double-space between column headings and the body.
Single-space content—double-space between sections if appropriate.

```
                    REVIEW OF INTERNATIONAL ACTIVITIES      line 7
                                    DS
                           Europe and Latin America
                                    DS
         Country                 Activity
                                    DS
         Ireland                 Emphasis on world-class manufacturing.
                                 Productivity good in all plants.

         United Kingdom          Creditable gain in profits.  However, margins
                                 unsatisfactory across divisions.

         The Netherlands         Satisfactory first half year; unsatisfactory
                                 second half.  Market share improved.  Quality
                                 improved.

         Italy                   Profits below last year; good foundation for
                                 new year.  Management revamped.

         Spain                   Strong foreign competition fuelled by weak
                                 dollar against an overvalued peseta.  Market
                                 offers potential for growth.

         France                  Strong market. New products introduced.
                                 Profits good.

         Germany                 Contributions good to overall European
                                 operations.  Representation changed.

         Colombia                Economic environment difficult.
                                 Representation unstable.  Sales unstable.

         Mexico                  Sales up.  Competition increased--domestic
                                 and international; prices adjusted to be
                                 competitive.

         Venezuela               Business unaffected by attempted coup.
                                 Markets improved.
```

REPORT FORMAT GUIDES

Use an unbound report format—1" margins on all pages except page 1.

For page 1, use a 2" top margin and 1" margins for sides and bottom.

Center the title in all caps.

Quadruple-space between the title and the body.

Double-space multiple-line titles.

Double-space above and below side headings and between paragraphs.

Use caps/lowercase and underlines for side headings.

Double- or single-space the body with double spacing between paragraphs.

Indent paragraphs.

Do not number the first page.

Number the second and remaining pages on line 7 at the top right margin; begin body a double space below the page number (on line 9).

2"

FUN & GAMES INTERNATIONAL DIVISION UPDATE

QS

The international market is now, and will continue to be, critical for Fun & Games' future. Approximately 55 percent of our business is from our international activities, and we see this percentage growing in the next ten years as a result of our commitment to expanding our international markets.

DS

During last year, international sales increased 18 percent over the previous year. This increase is significant because the stronger dollar depressed the exchange of foreign revenue. We achieved this success by entering new markets, adding product lines, developing new products, and improving our current product positions.

Expansion

Our existing operations in Italy, Spain, and Germany showed very strong increases during the year. And our expansion program continued on schedule with the addition of new subsidiaries in Hungary, Greece, and Mexico. FGI Hungary officially opened in September. To increase our market share in Greece, we completed our acquisition of the largest Greek toy manufacturer—El Greco—in October. FGI Mexico opened its doors in August. And we further showed our commitment to developing and serving the Pacific Rim markets by greatly expanding our Hong Kong marketing office.

Acquisitions

The acquisition of two additional product lines by our international operations went smoothly, despite a very complex process. While integration of new product lines has been handled differently in each country, consolidations of sales, marketing, and manufacturing resources, where appropriate, were largely completed during the year. The result is a more streamlined, efficient business that is ready for continuing growth in the future.

Games

The game business represents nearly 35 percent of total international sales. The classic games have proven to be valuable additions to our product portfolio.

Certainly we can be proud of our international record, but we are just beginning with many of these products. We plan to open operations to manufacture and market games in several new markets over the next five years. The Asia-Pacific region offers us particularly good prospects for development.

More information is on the next page.

REPORT FORMAT GUIDES (CONT.)

line 7   DS   2

    While we have been successful in the overseas marketing of games initially produced for sale in the U. S., we believe one of our competitive strengths is the ability to develop products for local and regional markets around the world. Next year, we will offer two new fantasy games to coincide with the opening of particular retail stores in Europe. The games are closely tied into European culture, so the products should sell well.

BLOCK-STYLE LETTER FORMAT

Use 1" or default margins.
Begin date on line 16 from top edge of paper.
Quadruple-space between the date and the inside address.
Use open punctuation.

Key the subject line in all caps without the word **Subject**.
Single-space the body.
Double-space between paragraphs.

FUN INTERNATIONAL GAMES
425 Fourth Street
P.O. Box 2000
Cincinnati, OH 45202-2000
513•555•3452 / 513•555•6350 (fax)

February 14, 19--   line 16

                                       QS

Señor Edgard A. Arana, Owner
CompuElectronics
519 De Diego Avenue
Puerto Nuevo, PR 00920
                                       DS

Dear Senor Arana

SERVICE CENTER AGREEMENT

Enclosed is the Service Center Agreement that we developed and discussed during my last visit. Please read it carefully and make any changes that you think are necessary.

Also enclosed is a list of questions to be answered by your office. They relate to your present setup and your future plans.

Please give me a call if you have any questions. I am looking forward to hearing from you soon.

Sincerely yours

                                       QS

Clarence Kupper
Vice President, Sales

hr

Enclosures: Service Center Agreement
            List of Questions

Block-Style Letter Format

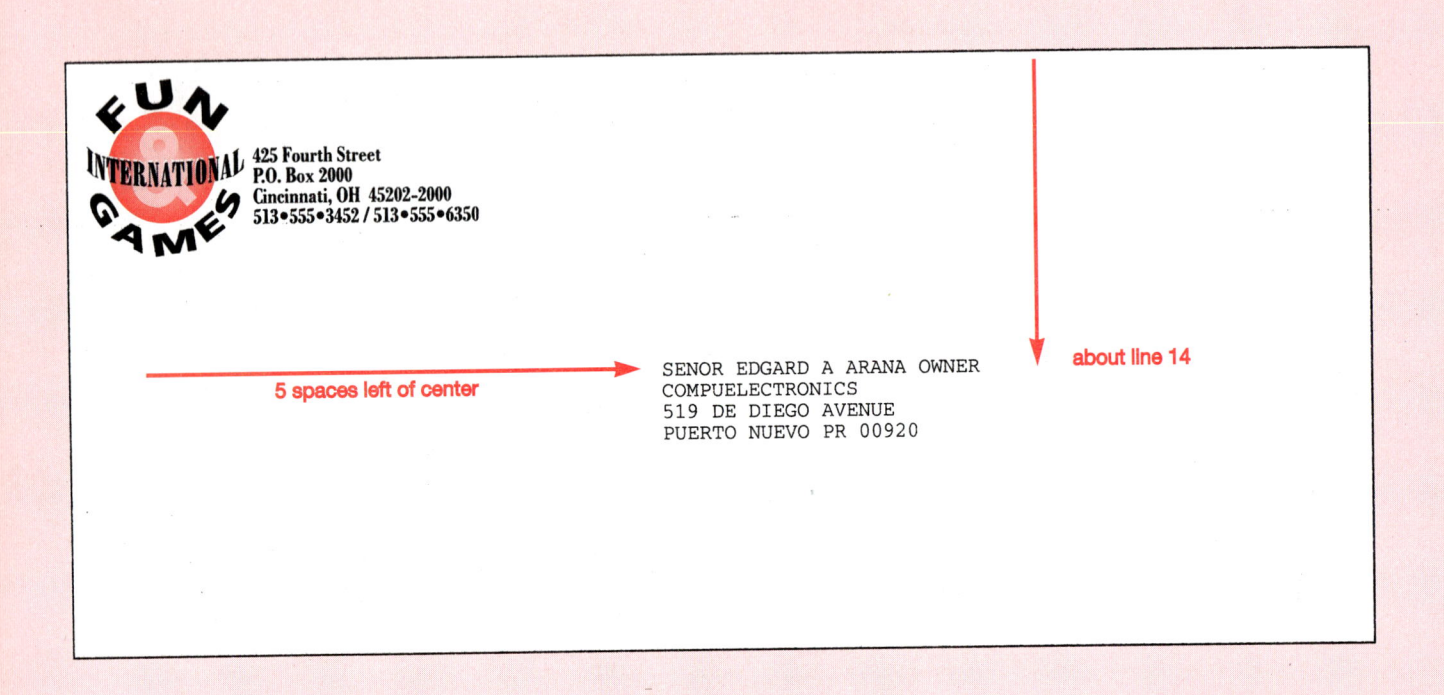

ENVELOPE FORMATS

Start on line 14.
Begin keying 5 spaces left of center of envelope.
Single-space address.

Key the information in all caps with no punctuation.

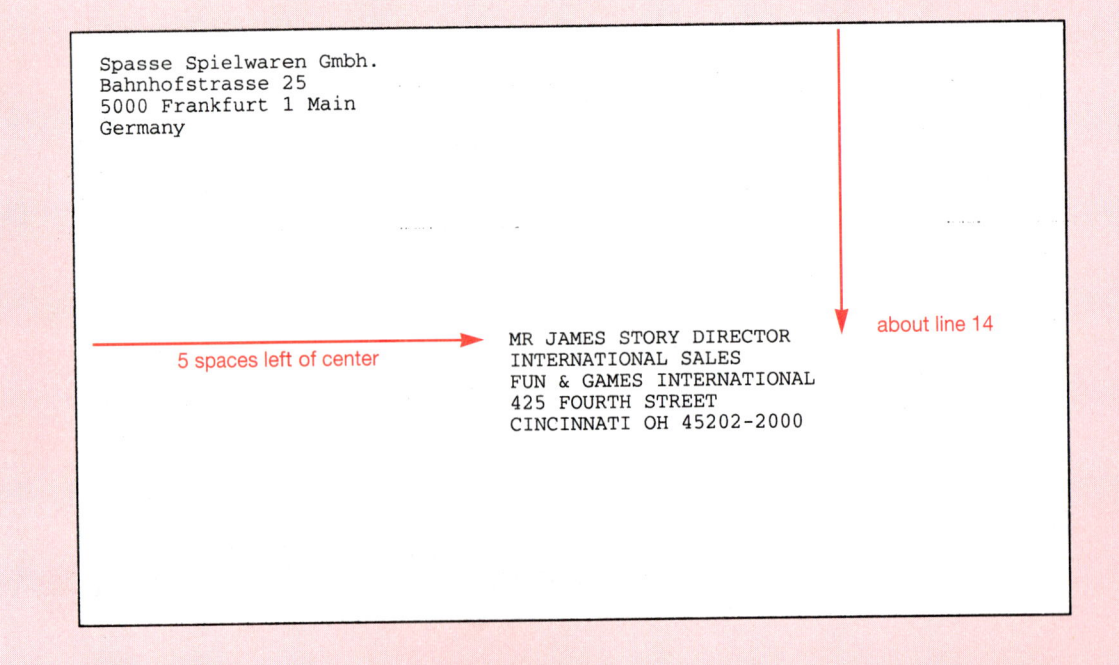

FUN & GAMES INTERNATIONAL
425 Fourth Street
P.O. Box 2000
Cincinnati, OH 45202-2000
513•555•3452 / 513•555•6350

```
                              SENOR EDGARD A ARANA OWNER        about line 14
5 spaces left of center  →    COMPUELECTRONICS
                              519 DE DIEGO AVENUE
                              PUERTO NUEVO PR 00920
```

Spasse Spielwaren Gmbh.
Bahnhofstrasse 25
5000 Frankfurt 1 Main
Germany

```
                              MR JAMES STORY DIRECTOR           about line 14
5 spaces left of center  →    INTERNATIONAL SALES
                              FUN & GAMES INTERNATIONAL
                              425 FOURTH STREET
                              CINCINNATI OH 45202-2000
```

INTERNATIONAL TIME ZONE CHART

Country	Country Code	Hours + or - Eastern USA Time
Argentina	54	+2
Australia	61	+16
Austria	43	+6
Belgium	32	+6
Brazil	55	+2
China	86	+13
Colombia	57	0
Costa Rica	506	-1
Denmark	45	+6
Egypt	20	+7
Ethiopia	251	+8
Finland	358	+7
France	33	+6
Germany	49	+6
Great Britain	44	+5
Greece	30	+7
Guatemala	502	-1
Honduras	504	-1
Hong Kong	852	+13
India	91	+10.5
Ireland	353	+5
Israel	972	+7
Italy	39	+6
Ivory Coast	225	+5
Japan	81	+14
Kenya	254	+8
Malyasia	60	+12.5
Mexico	52	-1
Netherlands	33	+6
New Zealand	64	+18
Nigeria	234	+6
Norway	47	+6
Peru	51	0
Philippines	63	+13
Portugal	351	+5
Saudi Arabia	966	+8
Singapore	66	+12.5
South Africa	27	+7
South Korea	82	+14
Switzerland	41	+6
Russia	7	+8
Taiwan	886	+13
Thailand	66	+12

International Time Zone Chart

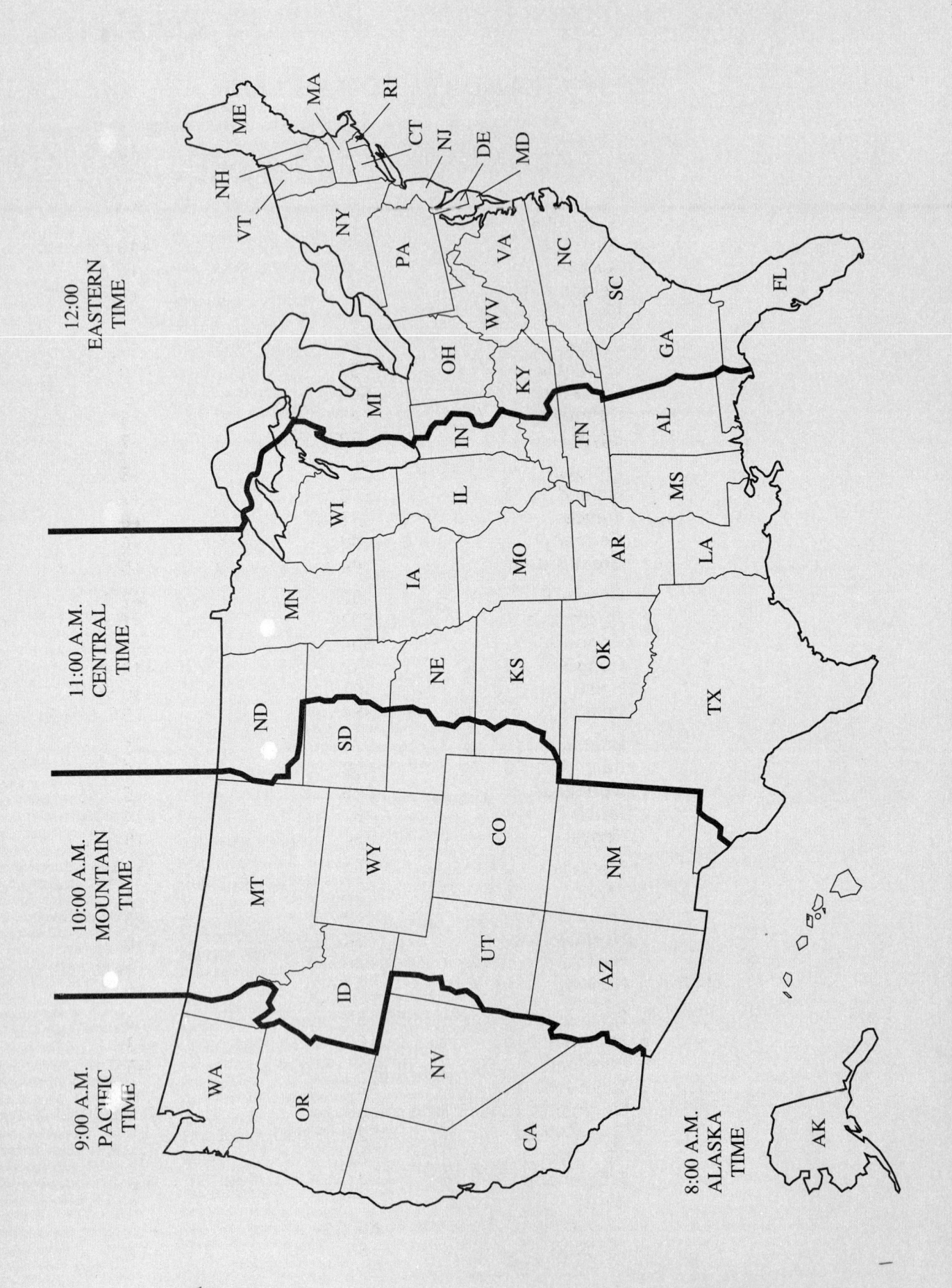